D0531820

SHORTHAND

ALEXANDER L. SHEFF

DICTATION
AND
TRANSCRIPTION

Speedwriting Publishing Company, Inc.
55 West 42nd Street, New York 36, N. Y.

NOTICE

"SPEEDWRITING" is the registered trademark of Speedwriting Publishing Company, Inc. and identifies the books and publications of that organization and the system of shorthand known throughout the United States and abroad under the term "SPEEDWRITING."

CENTURY EDITION

13

REVISED 1957

Printed in the United States of America

CONTENTS

Letters for Dictation 1

Tabulation 183

Special Techniques 200

Transcription 224

Mailing the Letter 273

GENERAL INDEX

A

a.m. (*A.M.*), 215
Abbreviations, states, 277
Address
  at end of letter, 264
  above date line, 265
  dropped inside, 264
  inside letter, 226
  on envelopes, 268
Addressing
  envelopes, 268
  letters, 226
Age, expressing, 214
Air mail
  notation, 268
  postage, 274
Ampersand (&), 221
Apostrophe ('), 220
Arithmetic method of tabulating, 191
Asterisk (*), 221
  in footnotes, 196
At sign (@), 221
Attention line
  in letter, 229, 251
  on envelope, 269

B

Backspace method of tabulating, 186
Block, standard letter style, 242
Body of letter, 230
Braced headings, 195

C

Capitalization, 202
Carbon copies, 203
  erasing, 206
  notation, 234
  pack, how to insert, 204

Care of notation, 217
Centering
  headings, 194
  vertical, 198
Cents (¢), 221
Certified mail, 275
Characters not on keyboard, 216
Cities commonly misspelled, 276
Close punctuation, 236
Colon (:), 218
Columns
  alignment of numbers in, 185
  arithmetic method of tabulating, 188
  backspace method of tabulating, 186
  headings for, 192
  one-column tables, 184
  two-column tables, 186
  more than two columns, 190
Comma (,)
  in numbers, 211
  spacing after, 218
Company name in closing, 231
Comparison of pica and elite, 183
Complimentary close, 231
Copies, carbon, 203
Copy notation, 234
Corrections
  carbon copies, 206
  erasing, 205
  reinserting paper for, 222
  squeezing, expanding, 207
Crowding in an extra letter, 207

D

Dash, 219
Date line, 225
Dates, how to express, 214
Decimals, 213
Degree sign (°), 216

Diagonal (/), 221
  use in fractions, 212
Dictator's name in closing, 232
Dimensions, how to express, 214
Distance, how to express, 214
Division of words, 200
Division sign (÷), 216
Dollar sign ($), 215
  in columns, 185
Double spacing, 230, 252
Dropped inside address, 264

E

Eliminating extra letter, 207
Elite type, 183
Enclosure notation, 233, 259
Envelopes, 268
Equal sign (=), 216
Erasing, 205
  carbon copies, 206
Erasure shield, 205
Errors, correction of (see Corrections)
Exclamation point (!), 216
Executive letterhead, 266
Expanding for correction, 208, 209
Extra letter, crowding in, 208, 209

F

Feet, inches, expressing, 214
Figures (see Numbers)
Firm name in closing, 231
First-class mail, 273
Folding letters, 272
Footnotes, 196
Fourth-class mail, 275
Fractions, 212
Full block style letter, 246, 253

H

Half-size letterhead, 267
Hanging indentation style letter, 261

Headings
  braced, 195
  centering, 194
  spacing of, 192
Hyphen (-), 219
Hyphenating words at end of line, 200

I

In care of, expressing, 217
Inches, feet, expressing, 214
Inch, number of spaces to, 183
  number of lines to, 183
Indented letter style, 248
Indenting for
  paragraph, 230
  numbered paragraphs, 230, 250
  quoted material, 231
In Re notation, 230, 250
Initials, reference, 233
Inserting
  carbon pack, 204
  letters into envelope, 272
  omitted letters, 207
Inside address
  above date line, 265
  dropped, 264
  in letter, 226
Insured mail, 276
Intercolumn spacing, 187
Inverted address, 264

L

Left parenthesis (( ), 220
Letters, folding and inserting, 272
Letters, parts of
  attention line, 229, 251
  body of letter, 230
  carbon copy notation, 234
  complimentary close, 231
  company name in closing, 231
    omitted, 231, 232
  date line, 225
  dictator's name and/or title, 232

enclosure notation, 233, 259
inside address, 226-228
letterhead, 225
postscript, 234
reference initials, 233
return address above date line,
 265, 270
salutation, 227
subject (*In Re*) line, 230, 250
Letters, placement chart, 238
Letters, punctuation forms
close, 236
mixed, 235
open, 237
Letters, special features
composed by typist, 252
numbered paragraphs, 231, 250
quoted material in body, 231
sender's address above date, 265
tabulation in body, 184
woman's signature in closing, 232
Letters, stationery used for, 225
Letters, styles
brief introduction, 240
full block, 246
indented, 248
informal business, 264
overhanging, 260
NOMA, 262
personal, 264, 265
semiblock, 244
standard block, 242
Letters, submitting for signature,
 271
Letters, two-page, 254-259
Line, typing on, 223

M

Made fractions, 212
Mailing instructions on envelope,
 268
Mailing the letter, 273
classes of mail, 273
Main heading, 192
Margins, 238

Married woman's signature in clos-
 ing, 232, 253
Mathematics, signs used in, 216
Measurements, expressing, 214
Minus sign (−), 216
Minutes and seconds, expressing,
 216
Missing letters, filling in, 207
Mixed punctuation, 235
Money, how to express, 215
Multiplication sign (×), 216

N

Notations
carbon copy, 234
enclosure, 233
on envelopes, 268, 269
Numbered paragraphs, 231
Numbers
alignment in columns, 185
in footnotes, 197
Roman, 213
rules for expressing, 209-213
summary chart, 214

O

o'clock, 215
Omitted letters, filling in, 207
Open punctuation, 237

P

p.m. (P.M.), 215
Page 2, 256
Paragraphs, 230
Parcel post, 275
Parentheses ( ), 220
Parts of letter (see Letters)
Percent (%), 221
Personal letters, 264
Pica type, 183
Placement of
address on envelope, 268
letters, 238
Plus sign (+), 217
Postage, 273-276

Postscript (*P.S.*), 234
Proofreader's marks, 278
Punctuation, marks of, 218
Punctuation, forms in letters, 235

Q

Question mark (?)
  spacing with, 218
  used with quotation marks, 219
Quotation marks ("), 218, 219
Quoted material in letter, 231

R

Raised numbers, 217
Rates, postal, 273
Re, 230, 250
Realignment of paper, 222
Reference initials, 233
Registered mail, 275
Reinserting paper, 222
Return receipts, 276
Right-hand margin, maintaining, 200
Right parenthesis ( )), 220
Roman numerals, 213
Rough drafts, 278
Ruled lines, typing on, 223

S

Salutation, 227
Second-page heading of letter, 256
Second-class mail, 274
Secondary heading, 193
Semiblock style letter, 244
Semicolon (;), 218
Shield used in erasing, 205
Slant (/), 221
Small letterheads, 267
Spacing
  columns, 187
  double, 230

envelopes, 268
headings, 192
punctuation, 218-221
Special delivery, 275
Special handling, 276
Spelling numbers, 209
Spreading to correct errors, 207
Squeezing to correct errors, 207
Standard block style letter, 242, 250
State abbreviations, 277
Straightening paper, 222
Subject line, 230, 250
Syllabication, 200
Symbols, 216

T

Tabulation
  braced headings, 195
  column headings, 193
  footnotes in, 196
  letters containing, 184
  main heading, 192
  on blank page, 198
  planning
    arithmetic method, 188
    backspace method, 186
  secondary heading, 193
  spacing between columns, 187
Third-class mail, 274
Time, expressing, 215
Two-page letter, 254-259

V

Vertical centering, 198

W

Weights and measures, expressing, 214
Woman's signature, 232, 253
Word division, rules for, 200
Words in letter, estimating, 238
Writing out numbers, 209

DICTATION COURSE

1

Mr. Charles R. Armstrong
546 Eastland Drive
Rochester, New York

Dear Mr. Armstrong:

In these days of prudent spending, we are inclined to practice economies that in reality result in waste.[2]

There is a time in the life of every automobile when the cost of upkeep far exceeds the value of[4] the service that the car can render. Today, new car prices are the lowest and new car values the greatest in the[6] history of the automobile industry. Take advantage of this opportunity to trade in your old[8] car for a new one.

The Crescent showroom is near your home and is open evenings for your convenience. Come[10] in and see the new Crescent Eight and enjoy a demonstration ride. Our representative will be glad to[12] explain our new easy-payment plan.

Sincerely yours,   (126)

2 lines

2

Buffalo Home Service Company
85 Prospect Street
Pine Bluff 4, Arkansas

Gentlemen:

We expect to be able to send the booklets requested in your letter of October 10 sometime during the[2] early part of next week.

We had hoped to have this unusual pamphlet, which is called PLANNING THE IDEAL KITCHEN,[4] ready on October 1. Our printer, who has been having production problems, told us yesterday that he will have[6] a small supply in our office on Saturday.

We are as eager to see the finished booklet as you are[8] because we know that the planning service in this publication is without doubt the best that has ever been offered[10] to home owners.

Yours very truly,   (106)

3

Trade Manufacturing Company
13 West 15 Street
Wilmington 17, Delaware
Gentlemen:

In order that you may learn about our newspaper, we shall send it to you free for a month. We hope that you will find[2] it interesting and helpful in your work. The news is reported in full in the "Post." The financial page will[4] keep you up to date on the stock market. We make it a point to include a full listing of all stocks.

Read the "Post"[6] for a month at our expense; then send us an order for daily delivery.

Yours very truly,　　　　　(74)

4

Messrs. Glover and Bradley
399 Asbury Avenue
Cleveland, Ohio
Gentlemen:

It gives me great pleasure to answer your inquiry of June 18 relative to the business ability[2] of Mr. John H. Sweet.

Mr. Sweet has been employed in our stenographic department for three years. I can[4] say that he has given ample evidence of being a hard and willing worker, accurate and dependable.[6]

He had had very little business experience when he joined our staff, but his persistence enabled him to meet[8] our requirements. It is with deep regret that we learn of his intention to change his position. We realize,[10] however, that this new opening offers opportunities in the field in which he intends to specialize.

I[12] know that you will find him an exceedingly valuable man.

Very truly yours,　　　　　(131)

5

Mr. Frank Close
37 West 144 Street
Albany, New York
Dear Mr. Close:

In replying to your recent letter, your order was delayed a short time because of the large amount of orders received. We have now added more men to our shipping room and additional orders from you will be shipped promptly.[4]

We hope to be of greater help to you in the future.

Very truly yours, (50)

6

Mrs. May House
23 North Street
Seattle, Washington
Dear Mrs. House:

We should like very much to get an order from you now since we are having our annual sale. This sale is not[2] advertised in the newspapers at the present time. Only our charge customers know about it. The public will not[4] be informed of the sale for approximately two weeks.

Most of our merchandise is included at significant[6] savings. In addition, a discount is offered for payment within ten days.

Yours truly, (74)

7

Lily Adams Dress Shops
580 Beaver Street
San Francisco 17, California
Gentlemen:

I am sure you will be pleased to learn that our company now stocks the dress material which you needed so badly[2] some time ago. As a result of your letter to us informing us of your needs, we sent to our dealers for[4] these goods and we

were successful in obtaining a large quantity in all colors. In
another envelope⁶ we are shipping samples of the colors.

If you are still in the market for the material, we shall be
glad⁸ to fill your order.

Yours truly,   (84)

8

Mrs. Helen Dawn
35 Westover St.
New City, North Dakota
Dear Madam:

The dress you ordered in your letter of April 4 comes only
in sizes 14 to 18. We do not have one² in size 11. This is not a
popular size and we shall have to write to our factory. In
addition,⁴ you wanted the dress in blue. We can give you the
same dress in black in size 11. If you can use the black dress,⁶
we shall hold it for you. If not, our factory will inform us
whether they make the dress in blue.

Please tell us your⁸ wishes as soon as possible.

Yours very truly,   (86)

9

Mr. Charles Brown
259 Oregon Avenue
Austin 17, Texas
Dear Sir:

Again we must ask you to settle your account, the balance of
which is shown on the enclosed bill. Although the² amount is
not a large one, you must realize that we cannot wait so long
for a check from you. The policy of our⁴ store with charge
customers is that all amounts must be paid in thirty days.

Please write us a check now so that it is⁶ not again overlooked.

Yours truly,   (64)

10

Mr. Fred Cunningham
218 Central Avenue
Pittsburgh, Pa.

Dear Sir:

In sending you the inclosed bill for three dollars for your subscription to the Alumnus, may I not urge you to² give this matter your immediate attention?

Our efforts to improve the alumni magazine have been⁴ undertaken in the belief that old and loyal friends would continue the support that they have extended so⁶ helpfully in the past.

All things considered, three dollars a year to maintain contact with your class, school, and university⁸ is not an unreasonable sum. This contact, together with the knowledge that you are cooperating¹⁰ in a worthwhile endeavor, should encourage you to renew your subscription.

Won't you draw your check for three dollars¹² now and mail it to us? Thank you.

Yours truly,   (126)

11

Stylewise Dress Corporation
935 Fourth Avenue
Pittsburgh 31, Pennsylvania

Gentlemen:

On September 1 I sent you an order for goods which should have been received by this time. What is the reason for² the delay in this shipment? This is the first time in our experience that orders from your company have been⁴ delayed in shipment. We need these goods for a special purpose and if we do not receive them in a few days, we shall⁶ be forced to cancel our order.

Uusally you have been most prompt in shipping our goods and we cannot⁸ understand this delay.

Yours truly,   (84)

12

Mrs. R. D. Stone
86 Morningside Drive
Watertown, New York
Dear Mrs. Stone:

Surprises await you at the new Wayside Gift Shop on Ridge Road.

We have a nicely appointed living room, a² dining room and a bedroom. In these rooms, gifts for the home are displayed in their appropriate settings. All gifts are⁴ individual in character and no duplicates are available.

On your last visit to our shop you⁶ inquired about a silver dish that might be used for flowers or fruit. We now have a handsome reproduction of⁸ an old Irish bowl in heavy silver plate that would admirably serve this purpose. The price of this attractive¹⁰ dish is $12 and we shall be glad to set it aside until you have an opportunity to call.¹²

Cordially yours,   (119)

13

Mr. Robert L. Miller
35 Main Street
Rochester, N. Y.
Dear Sir:

Because we want you to increase your paint sales we will print sales letters on your own stationery which may be sent² to your customers. We will do the printing, fill in the addresses, direct the envelopes and even pay the⁴ postage.

You will find that these letters will bring in good returns. We tried them last year for several dealers with such⁶ good results that we now want you to have the benefit of this advertising plan.

We are inclosing samples⁸ of the letters. Read them over and then send us your list of names and addresses as soon as possible so that¹⁰ we can start this work for you.

Very truly yours,   (105)

14

Miss May Blue
500 Stone Lane
Atlanta 17, Georgia
Dear Miss Blue:

We are sending you our catalog showing the materials we carry for summer covers. This material[2] is available for immediate delivery. We also enclose our price list. A discount of 10[4] per cent is offered for cash.

If you do not find the type of material you wish, may we ask you to come to[6] our shop where we have circulars from many houses in the city?

It is indeed a pleasure to be of service[8] to you.

Yours truly,   (81)

15

Miss Mary Black
Box 279
Suntown, Arizona
Dear Miss Black:

Thank you for your letter of March 10. It is a pleasure to write that your credit standing is good. You may order[2] goods on account with a 15 per cent discount in ten days, payment in full to be made in thirty days.

We hope[4] to receive your first order within a few days.

Very truly yours,   (49)

16

Miss Edna Sample
36 Lake Drive
Cleveland, Ohio
Dear Reader:

I am sorry to remind you of the sad fact that your subscription to our magazine has quietly expired.[2]

However, there is still time to prevent the calamity of your missing the next number. It is always a[4] calamity to miss an issue, for each one has a way of starting lively arguments and spirited talk,[6] not to mention the urge to independent thinking.

You have in your hand this minute a simple device that[8] reduces to a matter of seconds the time required for renewing your subscription. Simply tear off this sheet. You[10] will then have an envelope ready for mailing. Slip your check with the inclosed bill into it and the thing is done.[12]

Cordially yours,   (120)

17

Mrs. L. Locke
55 West 13 Street
Cleveland 15, Ohio
Dear Mrs. Locke:

Our records indicate that we have not received an order from you since last February. We have made many changes[2] in our store since that time, and we wish you would give us the opportunity to serve you again.

We carry[4] a new line of coats, dresses, and suits which I am sure are designed to please you. Look into the enclosed circular[6] and note our new low prices for these goods. Stop in and examine our stock when you are in town.

Yours truly,   (77)

18

Mr. Robert B. Drawn
307 West 23 Street
Centerville 5, New Jersey
Dear Sir:

Thank you very much for your check for $50. We have had no word from you since your check was received. Was there[2] anything wrong with our goods or our services?

If anything did not satisfy you in our recent shipment, please let[4] us know. We want you to be pleased with everything we offer.

Yours truly,   (50)

19

General Ink Company
91 State Street
Jersey City, New Jersey
Gentlemen:

The shipment of your X-92 ink received on September 2 is below standard according to complaints[2] received from schools in the last few days.

We have distributed this writing fluid under the Gladstone name for years as a[4] washable blue ink, which can be removed from clothing and furniture with soap and water. This product is[6] particularly popular in elementary schools, where the washable feature is a strong selling point.

Reports from[8] schools that have used bottles from your last shipment, however, indicate that something is wrong, and we are deeply concerned.[10]

We are sending you a sample from this shipment and shall expect a study of this matter and a prompt report.[12]

Very truly yours,   (121)

20

Messrs. Jones & Snyder
201 Proctor Street
Newark, N. J.
Gentlemen:

Thank you for your order of May 26 for two dozen watches amounting to $125.80.[2] We shall try to handle this order in such a way as will meet your approval and be the[4] means of further extending our business relations. A generous supply of our advertising material[6] will be shipped with your order.

The rules of all wholesale houses require that proper information be secured[8] before they extend credit. This information usually can be obtained from references. If you will[10] send us the name and address of your bank, we shall make the necessary inquiries as quickly as possible.[12]

May we hear from you by return mail?

Very truly yours,   (126)

21

Mrs. Janet Black
834 118 Street
Richmond 13, Virginia
Dear Madam:

Have you found the new book we sent to you interesting reading? Would you like us to send you additional books[2] which we feel you would like? The enclosed card is for your convenience in stating your wishes. If you would like a[4] book a month, please check where it is indicated. Perhaps you would only like to receive reports of new books[6] recently published and so decide for yourself which would interest you.

Drop the card in the mail so that we can be[8] of service to you.

Sincerely yours,   (84)

22

James R. Baker Company
62 Spring Street
New Haven, Connecticut
Gentlemen:

Inclosed is our booklet, WESTCHROME BRIDGE SETS, which will introduce our new line of tables and chairs for card games.

You will be[2] impressed by the strong construction of this furniture that has such smart style and is in good taste. A wide range of[4] colors and fabrics is available for chair coverings and table tops.

You should have several sets in your[6] stock because you would then be offering your customers the only bridge sets that positively resist wear and[8] retain their luster and richness for years.

Will you study this booklet carefully and let us know what set we may[10] send you for your inspection? You will not, of course, be obligated in any way.

Cordially yours,   (114)

23

Mr. Ronald M. Atkins
358 Pine Street
Portland 15, Oregon
Dear Sir:

Kindly mail me a check now for the balance due on your account. We do not get any pleasure in sending letters[2] like this to you, nor do we think that you like to receive them. However, in order for us to do business, we[4] have no choice in the matter but to make our position clear. I am sure you have to do the same thing from time to time[6] at your end.

We hope you give this letter immediate attention and that we find your check in the mail in[8] a very short time.

Yours very truly,   (84)

24

Hercules Desk Co.
27 Andover Lane
New York 25, New York
Gentlemen:

I notice that your account has recently been paid in full. We appreciate the prompt payment of our bills and[2] the opportunity of serving you.

Come in again and let us show you our new spring line.

Very truly yours,   (37)

25

Mrs. Robert Butler
1417 Chestnut Street
Reading, Pa.
Dear Madam:

In reply to your inquiry, we can furnish a boy's sweater in a blue and tan combination, size 12, for[2] $5.

Merchandise is sent on approval to customers who have charge accounts. We should be very glad to[4] number you among our charge patrons if you would favor us with the

usual bank and business references on[6] the enclosed card.
If you prefer, you may send us an order with a check
covering the cost. If the goods are not[8] satisfactory on delivery, you may return any article not desired, provided this
is done[10] within a reasonable time, and the merchandise is in
salable condition.

May we have the pleasure of[12] serving you?

Yours very truly   (122)

26

Miss June Blake, Secretary
Office Supply Company
47 River Street
Valley Stream, New York

Dear Madam:

I should like to secure a new adding machine for my office.
I would like you to mail me your latest price list.[2] Must I pay
the full cash price for this machine or do you offer a discount
to the trade?

I want a few days to[4] look over the catalog. Will you then
send a representative to talk to me about the various models[6]
and explain the advantages of each.

Truly yours,   (67)

27

Miss Louise Stewart
Central High School
Hartford, Connecticut

My dear Miss Stewart:

Miss May Black has applied for a position with our firm
and has given us your name as reference. We shall appreciate[2] it if you will express your opinion regarding Miss
Black, taking into consideration her ability[4] along general
lines, the initiative that she has shown in her school work,

and her inclination[6] to assume responsibility. When writing your letter, please consider also her character and her health.[8]

We will treat confidentially any facts that you may care to give us. If your letter is addressed to Box 20,[10] it will be delivered to me personally, in my private office.

We assure you that your cooperation [12] in this matter will be appreciated.

Very sincerely yours, (131)

28

New City Publishing Company
37 West 14 Street
San Diego, California
Gentlemen:

Your invoice of February 10 charged us for ten copies of your new book, "The Family Front." We have never[2] received the books nor do our records show that we sent you an order for them. However, from the advertisements[4] we have seen, we are interested in the book.

If you will ship us ten copies of the book, we shall send you a[6] check for the invoice. We shall, however, deduct our usual discount of 15 per cent.

Very truly yours, (75)

29

Mr. John R. Myers
25 State Street
New Hartford, New York
Dear Mr. Myers:

Thank you for your application for fire insurance which we received today from our agent, Mr. James Quinn. You[2] may be sure that we will make every effort to give you the best service possible under the terms of the[4] policy.

Inclosed is a binder to confirm your coverage. This is effective as of noon, January[6] 29, 1948. We are preparing a policy, which you will receive before the binder period[8] expires.

If you have any questions in regard to this insurance, or if we can be of further help to[10] you, please do not hesitate to call on us. We welcome you as a member of our insurance family.

Very truly yours.   (119)

30

Mr. Donald Drake
307 Maple Road
Camden, New Jersey
Dear Sir:

We regret that we must call your attention again to the balance of $35 which is now long past[2] due. The terms on which we open charge accounts is payment within a month. This amount is now three months old.

May we[4] look forward to a remittance from you not later than next week?

Sincerely yours,   (51)

31

Mr. Joel Fisher, President
Ace Electrical Company
34 West 17 Street
Reno, Nevada
Dear Sir:

It is indeed a pleasure to send Mrs. Gray to you for the position you mention in your letter of December[2] 4. She did very good work for us while she was in our employ. The only reason she left our company was[4] that she could not give us the hours we desired. Since she must look after her house, she wishes a part time position.[6]

Your offer appears to be her answer. She will see you on Monday.

Yours very truly,   (73)

32

Morrow Furniture Company
33 Washington Street
Springfield, Ohio
Gentlemen:

We welcome the opportunity to work with you in planning the reception room of the new office building[2] of the Hall Lumber Company.

Our Westchrome steel furniture will bring comfort and beauty to this very important[4] room. Complete information concerning our modern equipment appears in the catalog that is going out[6] to you today.

You will find styles and materials that fit every need and give charm to any interior.[8] No extra charge will be made for the use of more than one color because contrast in this regard is often[10] desirable. We shall be glad to suggest suitable color combinations if your customer is[12] interested.

Please let us know when we can help you.

Yours truly,   (128)

33

Mr. Robert Deal, Manager
City Sales Company
86 East 13 Street
Hoboken, New Jersey
Dear Mr. Deal:

After February 26 we shall move our office to 40 South Street in this city. We are[2] moving to meet the needs of our growing business in plastics. With more room, we feel we can be of greater service[4] to our customers.

It will take us a little time to get settled in our new quarters, but in the meantime[6] business will go on as usual. We look forward to receiving orders from you at our new address, and we[8] shall give our usual prompt service.

Yours very truly,   (86)

34

Mrs. George Harper
26 Second Avenue
Bridgeport, Connecticut
Dear Madam:

This is just a note of welcome.

We are pleased to learn that you have opened a charge account with us for we are[2] eager to serve people of discrimination. This account will prove a great convenience. It will make shopping much[4] easier and will give you a comfortable "at home" feeling.

We hope that when you visit the store you will be[6] interested in several of our new features, made possible by recent building additions. A department[8] devoted entirely to boys, another to girls, and a modern beauty parlor are a few of the attractions[10] which we hope will make your visits enjoyable. A cheerful tea room also has been provided for your[12] comfort while shopping.

Yours truly,   (123)

35

Mr. William P. Benton
Superintendent of Schools
Pearl River, New York
Dear Mr. Benton:

On November 15 we submitted a bid on the list of supplies which you sent to us on November 8.[2]

We know you will be glad to learn that changes in the paper market now make it possible for us to offer[4] you an extra discount of 10% on all paper items. We are inclosing a new proposal, therefore,[6] to cover your list with the request that you substitute it for the one submitted on November 15.

The[8] special discount of 2% on the entire order is still in effect.

We hope that favorable action[10] will be taken by your Board of Education at the meeting on December 14.

Yours very truly,   (116)

36

Mr. John Carey
873 Front Street
Toledo, Ohio
Dear Sir:

We have received your inquiry of January 17 in regard to the Webb Manufacturing[2] Company and are pleased to report that the concern is apparently in good standing.

Lately their business has[4] expanded rapidly and we are told that they are now operating as successfully as they did during the[6] war period. We understand that December was the busiest month in their history. Mr. Clark, the[8] president, has impressed us as a man of intelligence and ability. We consider him to be an able[10] executive. In local business circles he is credited with the rapid development of his concern.[12]

The above information should be considered confidential. We assume no liability in supplying[14] it.

Yours very truly, (141)

37

Charles A. Simpson, Inc.
12 Broad Street
Hudson, N. Y.
Gentlemen:

We are sorry to learn that you have been forced to replace a PA—45 hot water heater that[2] was installed less than a year ago.

Our guarantee provides that new parts will be supplied free of charge within one[4] year if a defect in manufacture is discovered. We have, therefore, asked Mr. Bond to inspect this heater[6] early next week. If he finds any evidence of manufacturing defects, you may be certain that the proper[8] adjustment will be made. The guarantee, of course, does not cover labor charges.

We regret the trouble you[10] have been caused and sincerely hope that Mr. Bond will clear up this matter to your satisfaction.

Very truly yours, (117)

38

Mr. Frank Jones
35 Oak Road
St. Paul, Minnesota
Dear Sir:

Our business has reached a new high! All orders receive prompt attention as soon as they are received. Have you[2] received our new catalog? In it is listed our complete line. Rather than wait for your reply, we are sending you[4] the catalog so that you can order for your spring needs. Goods that can be shipped by parcel post are shipped the same day[6] the order is received at no additional cost to you.

Please pass the catalog on to any of your friends[8] who are interested.

Very truly yours,   (84)

39

Mr. Harold Green
One West 3 Street
Chicago 2, Illinois
Dear Sir:

I have received your letter stating that you did not receive your last order. I have looked into the matter and[2] find that the books left our store in a regular shipment. I cannot understand the reason for the delay.[4]

However, we will send you another shipment. Should the first parcel arrive at a later time, please return it to[6] us at once.

Sincerely yours,   (62)

40

Mr. John Stone
15 West 59 Street
Richmond 14, Virginia
Dear Sir:

Your credit order No. 566 has not been sent as yet because we have not received the form we sent to[2] you. Before we ship

goods to a new customer, it is our policy to have this form
filled out. It is a simple[4] form and should not take you long to
fill out. List five credit references with whom you have done
business during the[6] past year and to whom we can refer. This
is the same method you would use with new customers.

As soon as we[8] receive the form, we shall make shipment.

Very truly yours,   (86)

41

Miss Alice Black
16 Allen Street
Albany, N. Y.
Dear Madam:

As requested in your letter of June 13, we are inclosing
folders giving rates and information[2] regarding our hotel.
Because of the popularity of our hotel, we shall be unable to
reserve any[4] room under $3 a day and for next month none
under $3.50 is available.

All[6] of our rooms are comfortably furnished and have hot
and cold running water. The hotel is located just one[8] block
from the station and within easy access to all parts of the city.

We shall be glad to serve you at any[10] time and suggest that
you write for reservations as far in advance as possible, so
that we can give you[12] the kind of room you want.

Yours truly,   (124)

42

Mr. John R. Bond
125 Market Street
Utica, New York
Dear Mr. Bond:

Thank you very much for placing your insurance business
with us. The policy inclosed is evidence of the[2] protection and
savings available to you.

We suggest that you review your policy carefully to make[4]
sure that it is written in accordance with your wishes.

Since the organization of our company, our[6] policyholders have always received liberal dividends, which have reduced the annual cost of their insurance.[8] The same low cost is available on other types of contracts purchased from us.

It is our desire to help you[10] in every possible way with your problems. If we may be of assistance to you, please call or write to us[12] at any time.

Cordially yours,   (123)

43

Mr. John Day
2 West 5 Street
High City, Vermont
My dear Sir:

We should like to inform you that we are opening a new store at 25 Stone Street. We will carry a full[2] line of coats, suits, and dresses. We also make these goods to measure.

Enclosed is a circular of our goods and prices.[4] Look it over. We are sure you will find it helpful when you are ready to buy.

Yours very truly,   (53)

44

Mr. George Press
37 G Street, Northwest
Washington 31, D. C.
Dear Mr. Press:

Thank you for sending me the report of the work done. We shall have it copied here in the office and return it[2] to you before the end of the month.

May I call your attention to the fact that the plant is now running at full[4] capacity and goods are being produced as rapidly as we get the material. We have not had any[6] labor trouble in over a year as the men are satisfied with their pay and working conditions.

These fine[8] conditions here mean that the government will get its orders with the least delay.

Respectfully yours,   (94)

45

Home Appliance Company
72 Lake Avenue
Buffalo 5, N. Y.

Gentlemen:

You emphasized a very important point when you stated that improper care and careless[2] operation of vacuum cleaners and carpet sweepers are increasing the demand for repair work.

Our service[4] department is preparing a booklet for distribution to owners of Ross equipment. The booklet will stress[6] the importance of proper care and correct operation as a daily measure. It will also illustrate[8] how simple repairs and adjustments can be made in the home.

A generous supply of these booklets will be sent[10] to you as soon as they are ready.

Very truly yours, (108)

46

Baker Brothers, Inc.
42 West Water Street
Dayton, Ohio

Gentlemen:

Our Mr. Burns has prepared a letter which we believe is suitable for your use in circularizing your[2] customers. A copy of this letter is attached for your criticism or approval.

We can multigraph a[4] supply of these letters on your own letterhead and send them to you ready to be filled in and signed. If you will[6] return the copy with your suggestions and send us the letterheads, we shall be glad to prepare the letters.

Our[8] plant is now operating on a schedule of five days each week. The office and factory will be closed on Saturday[10] until further notice. We shall, therefore, appreciate your cooperation in enabling us to care promptly[12] for your correspondence.

Yours truly, (125)

47

Mr. C. R. Clausen
84 Holbrook Avenue
Albany, New York
Dear Mr. Clausen:

During the past few months, we have had the pleasure of sending you various investment literature, which we[2] hope you found of interest.

It may be that you are holding some securities about whose future you are[4] uncertain, and which might possibly be exchanged for more promising issues. We shall be very glad indeed to have[6] you submit a list of your holdings on the inclosed form and to advise you concerning them. We have been helpful[8] to many clients in this respect.

Our statistical department is prepared to furnish opinions on any[10] securities you may own or may contemplate purchasing, and we cordially invite you to avail yourself[12] of this service.

Yours very truly,   (124)

48

Benson Glass Corporation
92 Fourth Avenue
Jersey City, New Jersey
Gentlemen:

We are interested in Benson jars because our wholesaler sent us a few cases late last summer and the[2] customer response was very good.

Our sales last year were far above the volume we expected. Consequently[4] we were forced to buy any type of jar that was available. Any jar could be sold last summer, of course, but[6] conditions will be different this season. Women are going to demand the jars that gave satisfactory[8] results. We do not expect to sell so many jars this year because many homes are well supplied now.

We plan to stock Benson[10] jars. Must we order from Jersey City or will your jars be available through the wholesalers?

Yours truly,　　　　　　(117)

49

Charles J. Walker and Company
125 State Street
Troy, New York
Gentlemen:

We were sorry to learn from your letter of June 16 that one of the MC-24 files shipped to[2] Emerson and Company was badly damaged when received.

We regret that we are not able to ship another promptly, and we know you will understand that this special color[4] job will take some time. The manager of the Finishing Department has assured us that work on this cabinet[6] will be rushed.

Will you please send another cabinet from your stock to help your customer until we are able[x] to replace the damaged file? We assure you that we shall be glad to make a satisfactory adjustment.[10]

Thank you for notifying us so promptly.

Yours very truly,　　　　　(108)

50

Messrs. Putnam & Smith
1990 Main Street
Rochester, New York
Gentlemen:

The other day we discovered something entirely different in the work of a real artist. It appealed to[2] our sense of humor and left us with a somewhat lighter spirit. We refer to the work of the English illustrator,[4] John Henry Wood, whose popularity is rapidly spreading.

It is with considerable pride that⁶ we announce the exclusive right to pass on to you twelve of Mr. Wood's humorous illustrations. One of these⁸ will reach you each month during the current year.

This is the first time the work of this artist has been released for¹⁰ advertising purposes in the United States. We hope that you will enjoy the pictures.

Read the inclosed circular¹² for further particulars.

Yours very truly,   (126)

51

New York Printing Company
270 Sixth Avenue
New York 14, New York
Gentlemen:

As you request in your letter of May 2, we enclose samples of our high grade bond paper in all colors. We² have been successful in selling this paper to many firms who wish fine paper for their letters. The samples⁴ represent the very best that we carry in stock and I am sure it will find favour by all who will use it.

Look the⁶ samples over carefully and decide which color is best for your purposes. After this is done, may we have⁸ your immediate order for the quantity you desire. It will go forward promptly.

Yours truly,   (96)

52

Messrs. Sanford & French
19 North Main Street
Buffalo, New York
Gentlemen:

We appreciate your substantial order of June 15.

We regret that the information in our reports² regarding your credit standing is inadequate. Your references speak highly of you but do not give the⁴ financial information that we consider necessary before making the first shipment on credit.

As[6] you are in immediate need of this merchandise, we suggest that you send us a bank draft. This will enable[8] you to take advantage of a four per cent cash discount instead of the usual two per cent. The cash[10] arrangement will apply to your first order only, as we are confident that future orders can be handled on[12] a satisfactory credit basis.

We await your reply.

Yours very truly, (131)

53

Mrs. Stanley L. Cosgrove
77 Parkwood Avenue
Rochester, New York

Dear Madam:

May we again send you our catalog? Last year we had the pleasure of sending you one of our publications,[2] and we hope that it has proved of value in your gardening efforts.

Our latest Seed Annual is now ready[4] and we shall be pleased to send it to you, if you are still interested in gardening. This book is a splendid[6] addition to any garden library; it contains valuable information, true-to-nature[8] illustrations, simple culture directions, as well as a complete list of dependable novelties in flowers,[10] vegetables, roses, and bulbs. You will find it a decided help in your garden plans.

An opportunity to serve[12] you will be appreciated.

Yours truly, (126)

54

James K. Watson
5 Farmington Avenue
Hartford, Conn.

My dear Mr. Watson:

In an endeavor to make our new Eight even more satisfactory, we have built at 30 Brown Place a new[2] service station, which we expect will be operated by our own employees. In this big, new, well-lighted[4] service station we are sure that we shall be able to service your car satisfactorily.

In so far as it[6] is possible, all repair work will be done on a flat-rate system, and the prices have been established by the[8] experts in the factory.

Kindly bear in mind that the location is the new building at 30 Brown Place and[10] that we have no connection whatever with any other service station in the city.

Very sincerely yours, (116)

55

Mr. R. D. Adams
515 Fifth Avenue
New York, N. Y.

My dear Mr. Adams:

As long as you are in good health you can provide for your family, but what would happen if you should have an[2] accident or be taken sick? Has this thought ever been brought home to you?

This company has recently issued a new[4] accident and health policy which provides protection for professional men. You pay us a small sum each month[6] or year, as you desire, while you are in good health and able to pay, and we pay you while you are disabled from any[8] cause.

If you are interested in protecting your family and yourself, I shall be glad to call at your[10] convenience and explain this policy in detail.

Very truly yours, (110)

56

Mr. F. J. Butler
111 State Street
Albany, New York

Dear Sir:

In response to your recent inquiry, we wrote you, quoting

prices on several units of radiator[2] furniture. We have not received a reply and wish to inquire whether you desire further details or whether[4] some of the information furnished is not clear.

It is our desire to make you fully acquainted with our radiator[6] equipment. We hope, therefore, that you have read carefully the descriptive folder that was sent you describing[8] Page furniture. The excellent design and construction of our product, as well as its general beauty[10] and utility, will undoubtedly add to the attractiveness of your home.

May we arrange to have our Mr.[12] Jones display one of our radiator covers in your living room?

Yours truly, (133)

57

Mr. Alfred E. Grant
Box 625
Warren, Arizona
Dear Sir:

It has been our custom in June and in December to send blanks to the secretaries of organizations[2] interested in advertising. Our purpose in doing so is to obtain a correct list of members to[4] whom we may mail our literature at regular intervals.

Our monthly bulletin presents current news of[6] importance to advertising concerns. We wish to compile a mailing list to which this publication may be[8] distributed for the purpose of stimulating interest in progressive advertising campaigns.

Will you[10] be good enough to fill out the enclosed blank, and place it in the stamped envelope and return it to us? We shall[12] appreciate your cooperation and we hope that we may be of service to you.

Yours truly, (136)

58

Mr. Thomas Seeley
59 Grant Avenue
Olean, New York
Dear Sir:

Your subscription to our magazine "Profits" expires in a little more than two months. All subscriptions not received[2] by expiration date are automatically canceled.

For your convenience, in order that you may not miss[4] any copies, we have taken the liberty of filling in your name on the enclosed renewal card. Simply sign[6] and mail the post card authorizing us to extend the subscription, and "Profits" will continue to reach you[8] regularly.

For only fifty cents more than the one-year price of "Profits," we will send you our improved budget book.[10] Read the enclosed circular describing this useful thrift device and then indicate on the enclosed card your[12] desire to have it.

Very truly yours,   (123)

59

Charles Crane & Company
28 Broad Street
Newark, New Jersey
Gentlemen:

We thank you for your check for $196 to cover your invoice of May 13.

On[2] examining our records, however, we find that a slight adjustment is necessary. The discount period,[4] during which two per cent could be deducted on this invoice, expired June 12. We are crediting you with the[6] amount of your check, which leaves an unpaid balance of $4 in your account.

You may feel that the small amount[8] involved in this particular case does not warrant our action. We wish to assure you that the same policy is[10] pursued with all our customers, regardless of how large or how small the account may be.

May we request your[12] cooperation?

Yours truly,   (123)

60

Modern Offices, Inc.
105 Michigan Avenue
Chicago 11, Illinois
Gentlemen:

We have your letter of June 15 in which you inclosed the specifications for the safe equipment to be[2] installed in the new offices of the Martin Manufacturing Company.

We shall be glad to send you pictures and[4] details of Western safes that meet these requirements.

It would be more convincing, however, to have you and your[6] customer visit us in Cleveland where our complete line of this heavy equipment is on display.

May we, therefore,[8] extend an invitation to you and your customer to come to Cleveland at our expense? Please telephone us[10] when it will be convenient for you, and we shall make the hotel reservations.

We hope to welcome you soon.[12]

Cordially yours,　　　　　　(120)

61

Mr. William Cooper
32 Maple Drive
Portland, Maine
Dear Sir:

We were glad to receive your request for our booklet, YOUR COMFORT AND YOUR HEALTH. A copy is inclosed with this letter.[2]

We hope you will let the Parker dealer in Portland, Mr. Robert O. Hall, 71 Church Street, help in[4] solving your heating problems.

He is prepared to study your needs, to supply the right equipment, and to provide[6] expert installation and service. His experience with local building and sanitation codes and his knowledge[8] of the fuel situation will make his advice valuable.

We are confident that our complete line of[10] products, plus the skill and experience of Mr. Hall, will give you many years of trouble-free heating service.

Yours very truly,   (119)

62

Miss Mary Hill
54 State Street
Troy, New York
Dear Madam:

It has always been the policy of this bank to encourage systematic thrift. In furthering this idea,[2] we are introducing a new dime carrier, which we should like you to try.

It may seem a small matter to put[4] in only a dime a day but the power of dimes is almost beyond belief. Dimes grow to dollars before you[6] realize it. The Woolworth Building was built with dimes. What we should like to have you do is to start the foundation of[8] a Woolworth Building and watch it grow.

Stop in the bank and allow us to lend you one of our dime carriers. You may have[10] your choice of several attractive leather covers.

Very truly yours,   (109)

63

Mrs. Joseph H. Norris
Riverview Apartments
Hudson, New York
My dear Mrs. Norris:

We have carefully examined the sweater that you submitted to us for credit. We find that the length of time since[2] the purchase and the condition of the garment prevent us from complying with your request. Our records indicate[4] that the purchase was made in April and our stock of these sweaters has since been closed out. We know that you will[6] appreciate the fact that, in our endeavor to give our customers only new and up-to-date merchandise, we[8] can not return to stock **a** garment that is no longer being carried.

We are making arrangements to send you[10] the sweater and we sincerely regret being compelled to refuse adjustment.

Very sincerely yours, (114)

64

Mr. William K. Hines
65 Warren Street
Syracuse, N. Y.

Dear Mr. Hines:

A fair profit in business can be earned many times but an unfair profit can be collected only once.

This[2] thought is the whole keynote of our policy of giving full value. We believe it is this policy that has[4] enabled us to achieve what authorities say is the greatest first-year success in hotel history. We[6] have found that more than half of our guests are sent to us by other guests. Surely the service that we render is[8] appreciated.

To help us give you even greater value, I hope you will tell us about any ideas that[10] will make this a more enjoyable home for you on your next visit to this city.

Sincerely yours, (114)

65

Adams Heating Service
83 Bridge Street
Buffalo 6, N. Y.

Gentlemen:

We are sending you a supply of booklets that will explain to your customers how simple it is to modernize[2] their homes now with Parker equipment.

The easy monthly terms of the Parker Financing Plan will spread the payments[4] over a long period while the comfort and savings resulting from the improvements are being enjoyed[6] by the family.

We shall be glad, of course, to work out time-payment programs to meet the needs of special cases[8] that are not covered by the standard plans.

We are eager to do everything we can to bring comfort and[10] economy to the homes of your customers because we believe modern homes are the best investment in the nation.[12]

Yours very truly,   (121)

66

Mr. Joseph Adams
426 Pine Street
Utica 4, New York
Dear Mr. Adams:

We have learned that you will soon take delivery on a new car. We should like to arrange insurance on this car[2] against driving risks.

Our policies include liability for bodily injury and property damage[4] as well as loss caused by fire or theft. You can also have insurance against damage to your own car, which can be[6] obtained on a $25, $50, or $100 deductible basis. This means that, depending upon[8] your policy, we will pay the repair bills in excess of the amounts mentioned.

Our Mr. Quinn will call on you[10] soon to explain our services. He will quote the rates on the various forms of protection available.

Yours truly,   (119)

67

Messrs. Lane & Benson
144 Union Street
Trenton, N. J.
Gentlemen:

We have before us your recent inquiry concerning the operation of our Circular Letter Department.[2]

Our first duplicator, purchased about eight years ago, was used for form letters only, but the department[4] has been reorganized and we now use seven of your machines. These handle not only our form letters, but also[6] about twenty per cent of our printing as well.

Our records show a saving of twenty-five per cent on all[3] printing done by this department as compared with the cost of outside work, and a decrease of forty per cent in[10] the cost of forms.

We consider that your machines are actual dividend producers and take great pleasure in[12] recommending them to any business organization.

Yours very truly,   (131)

68

Mrs. Robert Watson
24 Hillcrest Avenue
Providence, Rhode Island
Dear Mrs. Watson:

Each season, Marie plans collections of clothes specially for the college girl and each year an additional[2] number of smart women, in and out of college, are finding here just the things they most desire.

The growing popularity[4] of these gay, youthful fashions prompts us to suggest to all our customers the advisability of[6] looking at them when planning spring wardrobes. They are being first shown this week.

This season, the mode offers such variety,[8] such individuality, and the market such splendid values, that we are sure that you will want some of our[10] selections.

The inclosed folder has been made complete in illustration and description so that you can conveniently[12] order by mail or telephone.

Cordially yours,   (127)

69

Mrs. Walter L. Graham
209 North Avenue
Scranton, Pennsylvania

Dear Madam:

We are very glad to send you a copy of our booklet, "The Care of Children." We believe you will get much[2] practical help from it.

For thirty-three years food experts have recommended our product as the first solid food for[4] babies and as the hot cereal that every growing child should have for breakfast. It is a wonderful[6] energy-producing food and is in such simple form that it can be digested quickly and easily.

Please try[8] some of the delicious recipes suggested in the booklet. Not only the children, but also the whole[10] family, will enjoy them. They add welcome variety to the daily menu and are easy and economical[12] to prepare.

Yours very truly,   (124)

70

Mr. Robert S. Anderson
Public Waterworks
Washington, D. C.

Dear Sir:

For some time we have been in the habit of following up all breaks in the water mains. We hope to obtain[2] information that will assist us in the manufacture of cast-iron pipe and in the prevention of similar[4] breaks in the future.

We understand that a six-inch main recently broke near the corner of Rhode Island[6] Avenue and 17th Street in your city. If consistent with your practice, will you kindly furnish us some[8] general information regarding this break and its cause, as determined by your department? Just fill in the[10] attached blank and return it to us.

We hope that you will consider us at your service whenever we can be[12] of help.

Yours truly,   (121)

71

Dr. Edward W. White
Superintendent of Schools
Lewisburg, Pennsylvania

Dear Dr. White:

We were sorry to learn from your letter of December 20 that four dozen pint jars of Duro paste are missing[2] from your order No. 342.

Our records show that this order was delivered by the Emerson Trucking[1] Corporation on November 15. The receipt signed by James E. Kennedy at the Wilson High School[6] claims no shortage. You will understand that it will be difficult now to trace the missing items because of the[8] time that has elapsed since delivery.

We realize, however, that your teachers need this paste in their classes, and[10] we are eager to cooperate. A duplicate shipment is therefore being sent today by express.

Yours truly,   (116)

72

Messrs. Evans & Brown
157 Dearborn Street
Chicago, Ill.

Gentlemen:

We are pleased to inform you that the Bonus Wage Plan as installed in our plant by your engineer, Mr. White, is working[2] out satisfactorily. It has stimulated our production and appears to be a flexible means[4] of handling the wage-payment problem. Even better results will be obtained when our foremen and factory hands[6] become thoroughly familiar with the operation of the plan.

We take this opportunity to state that[8] your engineer directed the installation of the system in a very satisfactory manner. He[10] was courteous and diplomatic in making suggestions and obtained the respect of our employees.

We shall[12] write you again regarding our progress under your Bonus Wage Plan.

Very truly yours,　　　(132)

73

Mr. Charles Grover
Packard Building
Philadelphia, Pa.

My dear Mr. Grover:

I have looked further into the gray lumber situation and have learned that, although earnings may not be sufficient,[2] the interest charges on the first mortgage will be paid.

The directors of this company are honorable[4] men with strong financial standing. The property, also, is apparently good. Although there have been difficulties[6] in meeting payments on the principal, the interest charges have been and will continue to be paid[8] regularly.

I have been informed by a reliable source that a report of earnings has been made, but up to[10] the present time I have been unable to procure a copy for you.

I will talk to you further about this matter[12] when I see you.

Cordially yours,　　　(124)

74

Mr. Ralph A. Winslow
89 Grandview Avenue
Portland, Maine

Dear Sir:

We are glad to send you a copy of the radio address of Mr. Howard Clark, president of the[2] National Association of Savings Institutions, which you recently requested.

It is a pleasure to[4] learn that you are listening to our radio hour and we hope that you will find the programs sufficiently[6] enjoyable to "tune in" every Wednesday evening. The radio talks cover a variety of[8] investment subjects which not only are interesting in themselves but also will be of real help to you in building[10] a strong investment account.

If at any time you have specific questions to ask regarding bond investments,[12] we shall be very glad to have you write to us.

Very truly yours,   (129)

75

Strong Brothers
238 Lake Street
Newark 3, N. J.
Gentlemen:

We were pleased to learn from your letter of January 18 that you are planning to submit a bid for the[2] plumbing and heating requirements of the new Green Valley Hospital. You may be sure of our complete cooperation.[4]

The manufacture of this equipment involves problems that we have been studying for years. Fixtures must[6] stand up under rough service twenty-four hours a day, year after year. Parker products are designed to meet special[8] needs, and all materials have been time-tested in actual hospital use.

We shall be glad to have our planning[10] division help you in preparing your bid. We suggest that you let us send a trained engineer to your office.[12]

Yours truly,   (121)

76

Mr. James S. Martin
136 Commonwealth Avenue
Boston, Massachusetts
Dear Mr. Martin:

There are several reasons for the excellent showing of this bank during the past year. In spite of unfavorable[2] economic conditions generally, we have maintained large deposits and a thoroughly sound[4] financial position.

While this has called for courage, and careful management on the part of officers and[6] directors, we believe that a large share of the credit should go to our depositors. Their cooperation and[8] unfailing friendship are among our strongest resources. To all of these friends and to you personally, we[10] express our thanks.

We look forward with confidence to a prosperous future based on the industry and intelligence[12] of the people of our country. May you abundantly share in this prosperity.

Cordially yours,   (136)

77

Mr. George Bliss
255 West Avenue
Rochester, New York
My dear Mr. Bliss:

The inclosed discount card entitles you to a discount on all purchases at this store.

For years we have specialized[2] in silver, carrying all standard makes and patterns in both sterling and fine plate. You will find in our display[4] many gift suggestions suitable for every occasion and covering a wide range in price.

If you have[6] in mind any particular article not regularly carried in stock, we are prepared to make it up[8] on your order at a reasonable price.

With your discount card you can secure a substantial reduction in[10] the cost of your purchases. There is no time limit on the card. Use it as frequently as you desire.

Very truly yours,   (119)

78

Mrs. James Wright
45 James Street
Boston, Massachusetts

Dear Mrs. Wright:

Is it the fault of this store that your account remains inactive?

I am deeply concerned that you have ceased to use[2] your credit privilege with us. We appreciate the importance of keeping old friends, and if through any fault of ours[4] you are not using your account, I hope you will let me know personally.

Our policy is to give complete[6] satisfaction. If we have failed in any way, I shall regard it as a favor if you will write me a[8] letter telling me the cause of your dissatisfaction. Smith & King will welcome an opportunity to[10] prove that they value and appreciate your patronage.

May I hear from you?

Very cordially yours, (114)

79

Mrs. J. L. Brown
84 West Avenue
Utica, N. Y.

Dear Madam:

The approach of warm weather suggests sending your furs to storage to be cared for during the hot summer months.

Fire,[2] theft, moisture, moths—none of these can touch your furs in our specially constructed cold storage vaults. Here furs are protected[4] during the summer months and returned to you in the fall in perfect condition.

Your fur coat may be a[6] little worn or need a new lining, or it may need to be remodeled. By having this attended to now you[8] receive the benefit of prices much lower than in the fall or winter.

Just write or telephone when you are ready[10] to send your furs to storage and our messenger will call.

Yours truly, (111)

80

Anderson Hardware Company
295 Broadway
Yonkers, New York
Gentlemen:

Since experience has proved that angling contests sponsored by local dealers are one of the best methods of creating[2] interest in fishing, we urge you to study the plans
outlined in the inclosed booklet. You will find complete[4] information concerning organization, publicity, and rules.

You may send your program, if you decide[6] to use this type
of sales promotion, to Mr. William Haines of our Contest
Department for suggestions. His long[8] experience in this
field should be most helpful.

We want you to feel that we are always interested in any[10]
plan you may devise to increase your sales. Your problems
will always become our problems as soon as you write us.[12]

Yours very truly, (122)

81

Mr. Joseph Nichols
Sporting Goods, Inc.
81 Pine Street
Atlantic City, New Jersey
Dear Mr. Nichols:

Progressive dealers all over the country are increasing their
volume of quick sales by the use of Walker[2] window and
counter advertising.

These beautiful displays are described in the inclosed booklet, SILENT[4] SALESMEN AT WORK. Some of these color-

ful reminders in your store will enable you to take advantage of our[6] regular program of national advertising.

Why not send us a list of the materials that will help[8] you move your stock?

We should also be glad to receive your suggestions for additions to this group of display cards.[10] Many of the best ideas come to us from the men behind the counters who really know the needs of fishermen.[12]

Yours very truly,   (122)

82

Miss Mary King
25 Mill Street
Utica 2, New York
Dear Miss King:
We acknowledge your request for a change in your automobile insurance policy. This contract will be[2] extended to cover your new 19— Rocket Sedan, motor[4] No. 15287.

If this information is incorrect, kindly notify us at once. The change is[6] effective as of twelve noon, January 29, 19— and your new car will be protected in accordance[8] with the provisions of the original policy. A rider covering this change in insurance will be[10] sent to you soon.

Would you be interested in considering the addition of collision insurance[12] to your coverage? Mr. Quinn will be glad to explain this type of protection to you.

Yours truly,   (138)

83

Buffalo Home Service Company
85 Prospect Street
Pine Bluff 4, Arkansas

Gentlemen:

Since our factory has completed its government assignment, we are making every effort to get back to[2] the manufacture of kitchen and laundry equipment for homes.

You will be pleasantly surprised to know that we[4] shall be able to include in our new line many improvements that we once thought would have to wait for several[6] months. The gradual change-over from government work that started last spring has made this possible.

A splendid new[8] booklet on home planning will soon be ready for your customers. The women who use kitchens and laundries know how they[10] should be equipped and arranged. In preparing this material, therefore, our engineers consulted thousands of[12] housewives.

                                   Yours very truly,   (123)

84

James A. West and Company
17 Morrison Avenue
Newark, New Jersey

Gentlemen:

Although we have been making plans for a long time for low-cost home building, we must now speed up our preparations.

The[2] building of new homes and the improvement of old homes will be the natural result of the release of building[4] materials and labor. A heavy demand for home equipment and fixtures is just ahead and we wish to[6] be ready to meet these needs.

We were glad to learn that you are preparing a new booklet on the planning of[8] modern kitchens. Please send us a supply for our customers as soon as possible, and keep us informed from time[10] to time concerning the equipment and fixtures that become available.

Yours very truly, (115)

85

Atlas Storage Company
300 Madison Avenue
Albany 3, New York
Gentlemen:

Mr. Charles Lee of White Plains, New York, has consulted with me in regard to the damages that he sustained as the[2] result of a recent automobile accident. A truck owned by you and operated by your driver, John[4] Adams, was involved. The collision occurred March 2, on Route 9, near the village of Hyde Park, New York.

This accident,[6] which resulted in the death of Mrs. Lee, was caused through the negligence of your driver. Mr. Lee, therefore, expects[8] to be compensated for his loss.

I suggest that you turn this letter over to your insurance company[10] so that the company may have a representative call at my office to discuss the matter.

Yours truly,[12] (120)

86

Mr. Joseph W. Lee
22 Grand Avenue
Yonkers 6, New York
Dear Mr. Lee:

Your father has filed a petition in the Surrogate's Court that he be appointed administrator of your[2] mother's estate. Your brother Harry and your sister Jane have signed waivers, consenting to this appointment.

I[4] assume it is agreeable to you that your father be appointed administrator. I am, therefore,[6] enclosing a waiver for you to sign so that it will not be necessary to have special papers issued[8] and served upon you.

Sign the form before a notary public and return it to me in the inclosed stamped[10] envelope. Please do this promptly so that we may proceed with various matters in connection with the estate[12] that must await your signature.

Yours truly,   (135)

87

Mr. Charles Lee
600 Central Avenue
White Plains, New York
Dear Mr. Lee:

I have obtained the bond that you, as administrator of the estate of your wife, must file with the Surrogate's[2] Court. Inclosed is the application, together with the original and two copies of the bond.

Please fill[4] in with care the information requested in question 5 of the application. You may estimate the[6] amount of cash that you have and your liabilities, if any.

Sign the application, together with[8] original and the two copies of the bond, in the spaces marked X, in the presence of a notary[10] public.

The prompt return of all the inclosed papers will enable me to proceed immediately with the[12] settlement of the estate.

Very truly yours,   (128)

88

Mr. Charles Lee
600 Central Avenue
White Plains, New York

Dear Mr. Lee:

I am inclosing a form in order to have the Savings Bond that was in your wife's name alone reissued.[2] After this paper has been signed by you in the presence of a qualified official, kindly return it to[4] me immediately.

You will note that I have provided that the bond is to be issued in your name as[6] administrator. It is not possible on this request to have the bond issued in any other form. If you[8] wish to name an additional individual on the new bond, you will have to file a separate request.[10]

This will conclude the transfer of all the bonds that were in your wife's name.

Very truly yours,   (115)

89

Mr. Charles Brown
46 School Street
Buffalo 12, New York

Dear Mr. Brown:

Welcome to Buffalo! We understand that you and your family plan to live here. We know that you will find our[2] city a pleasant and friendly place in which to work and live.

Our business demands that we keep closely informed about[4] local conditions. If there is anything Lane Brothers can do to help you in getting settled, please come in and[6] let us know. We may be able to give you a helping hand in a number of ways.

You will, no doubt, wish to establish[8] credit in a local department store now that you are a resident of this community. If so, we[10] invite you to open an account with us.

Cordially yours,   (110)

90

To whom it may concern:

This is to bear testimony concerning the sterling qualities of Miss Virginia Blank, who is now[2] assistant in English at Columbia University.

Miss Blank is twenty-three years old. She is a high-school[4] graduate and took her A. B. degree at the Syracuse University last June 23. Miss[6] Blank was appointed assistant in English in the Summer Session at Columbia University last[8] July; and she was reappointed, as a result of her good work, for the September 15 term.[10] During the past year she has worked directly under my supervision and I thus feel competent to[12] express an opinion concerning her ability, character, and performance that should have weight with any[14] prospective employer.

She comes from an exceptionally good family and possesses the characteristics[16] of a lady brought up in refined circumstances. During her year at Columbia, I found her services[18] invaluable. She has assisted me in giving a course in Business English, and I have found her not only[20] above the average in intelligence, but also serious, thoughtful, and conscientious. She has shown much[22] initiative and executive ability. I am sure if Columbia University loses[24] her services it will be with many regrets by all who know her. If she leaves the University, it[26] will be of her own accord, and because she wants to engage in work where she can make her personality more[28] effective than she can in occupying a subordinate position in a great university.

While[30] Miss Blank is young, she is not a chit of a girl; and I am convinced that she will fill with dignity and efficiency[32] any position which she accepts. I commend her most cordially to any one requiring the services[34] of a competent teacher.

(346)

91

Mr. George A. Stockholm
Bentley High School
Danbury, Connecticut
Dear Mr. Stockholm:

Hundreds of teachers are making daily use of our recent publication, Modern Dictation. It seems to fill[2] exactly the need of a real book for homework.

Five or six letters are assigned for each night. The pupils practice[4] the new words listed in the lesson. Then the complete letters are written in shorthand two or three times to secure[6] ease of writing and to increase the shorthand vocabulary. The next morning these same letters are used in class[8] by the teacher for dictation in building up speed.

We consider this program ideal for the pupil in[10] advanced dictation. Does this plan appeal to you?

May we send you a complimentary copy of Modern Dictation?[12]

Very cordially yours, (121)

92

Fairfield Hardware Company
33 Simpson Street
Hudson, New York
Gentlemen:

We were happy to learn from your letter of April 4 that your experience with Benson jars was so[2] satisfactory.

We urge you to place your order early, because the demand will be heavy again this summer. Your wholesaler[4] will be able to obtain Benson canning supplies, so it probably will be more convenient for you to place your[6] order there.

Very truly yours,　　　　(61)

93

General E. F. Church
145 Fifth Street
Albany, New York
My dear General:

Some years ago I bought a home in the country for my children. At the time I bought the place there was much work to be[2] done on it.

The house was about to fall down, but it is now in perfect repair. The garden, which was more than a[4] hundred feet drop, was running wild with all kinds of flowers. That, too, has been all done over, and it is a beautiful[6] spot to look at.

The large field in which the children used to play runs right up to a fine bit of woodland, and on[8] the other side of it there is a high mountain from which one may get a beautiful view of the country for[10] miles around.

My children have now grown to be young men and women, and they like the seashore better than they do the[12] country. For this reason I am offering the place for sale on very easy terms.

I think your little ones would[14] love the place just as my babies did, and I can think of no one I would rather have it than you.

If you would like[16] to buy it, I am sure we can meet on the terms. Will you let me hear from you soon?

With kind regards to Mrs. Church,[18] I am,

Your friend,   (182)

94

Western Form Supply Company
13 West Flower Road
Tulsa, Oklahoma

Gentlemen:

Knowing that you employ a large corps of bookkeepers and office assistants in your establishment, I respectfully[2] apply for a position as bookkeeper.

I am twenty-two years old, was brought up on a farm, and with[4] the exception of the past two years have always lived in the country. Two years ago I graduated from Eastman's[6] Business College, taking the degree of Master of Accounts. Since graduation I have been employed in this[8] city. For the first six months I was with the Produce Exchange Bank, corner of Third Avenue and 116th[10] Street. During the past year I have been employed by the Guardian Trust Company, 170[12] Broadway. I left the Produce Exchange Bank to better myself with the Guardian Trust Company. As there seemed[14] to be but little opportunity in the banking business, I terminated my connection with the[16] Guardian Trust Company on March first. My record with both banks, I believe, is good, and I am permitted to[18] refer to them as to my faithfulness and reliability.

I am large in stature, strong, healthy, and unmarried.[20] My training has been such as to fit me especially to take up any ordinary set of books and keep them[22] according to the most approved modern methods. I realize that I am a young man, and I am very desirous[24] to succeed. Wherever I am employed I expect to earn my money; and I am willing to work hard and[26] put in long hours. My employer's interest shall

always be mine, and I shall do all in my power to serve him[28] faithfully.

I have no bad habits, keep regular hours, and try to be pleasant and obliging to all. While I[30] am especially fitted for a bookkeeper's position, I feel that I can do many other kinds of work[32] that a handy man might be called on to do in a business office.

Should you be able to use such a man in[34] any capacity, I shall be glad to begin with you at a salary of $50 a week. I[36] believe I can "make good."

I hope you have a vacancy for such a man.

Yours sincerely,   (373)

95

Bruce Book Store, Inc.
95 Dearborn Avenue
Pittsburgh, Pa.
Gentlemen:

An examination copy of *Your Health and Your Food* is in the mail. Read it and we know you will agree with us[2] that at last the relation of food to health appears in language that can be understood by everyone.

This book[4] is full of useful information but technical terms have been avoided. The author has no product to sell[6] except health and happiness.

Yours truly,   (66)

96

Messrs. Blank & Blank
250 West 57 Street
Concord, Massachusetts
Gentlemen:

One good turn deserves another. I did YOU one today, and I am sure you will reciprocate as soon as you[2] know about it.

As I entered the credit department this morning, I noticed on the desk of the credit man[4] several accounts which he was about to send to the Collection Department of CLOAK, SUIT, AND SKIRT MANUFACTURERS'[6] PROTECTIVE ASSOCIATION. Seeing your account among them, I remarked,

"This will never do. There must[8] be some mistake about this. Messrs. Blank & Blank are accustomed to paying their bills. Hold that account until I write[10] the firm a personal letter. I can't consent to have even a suspicion of unreliability[12] cast upon so good a customer."

Now that you know my attitude, I trust you will look at this letter in the[14] spirit in which it is written,—a spirit of business friendship and protection.

Your over-due account amounts[16] to $750. I need this money at once. Will you not do your utmost and send me a check[18] by return mail. By so doing you will prove my contention that my customers are my best friends.

Yours truly,   (197)

97

Buffalo Home Service Company
85 Prospect Street
Buffalo 12, New York

Gentlemen:

We are inclosing a complete list of the kitchen and laundry equipment that is available at this time. The[2] supply is, of course, limited at present but we shall do our best to make certain that each dealer has[4] an opportunity to obtain a fair share.

You will be glad to see that several new pieces of laundry equipment[6] are included in this list. These modern appliances may be used in planning a new kitchen or in planning a[8] separate laundry room.

Yours very truly,   (87)

98

Mr. George A. Stockholm
Bentley High School
Danbury, Connecticut
Dear Mr. Stockholm:

Have you ever seen as good a selection of graded material as that provided in Modern Dictation?[2]

More than five hundred letters and many interesting articles and speeches fill this book to the brim. This[4] is the type of material that will help you to make capable stenographers of your pupils. At the rate[6] of five letters and one article a day, you will cover in one term a range of business literature that[8] will prepare the members of your classes for effective stenographic service.

Modern Dictation does not take[10] the place of any of the standard shorthand textbooks. It is intended solely for use in advanced classes. It[12] is an ideal finishing book.

Very cordially yours,   (126)

99

Miss Mary L. Lowell
1056 University Avenue
Cambridge, Massachusetts
My dear Miss Lowell:

The Watson Jewelry Company of Boston has informed us that you have selected the Fairfield as your[2] pattern of silver. We congratulate you on your choice. The Fairfield is certainly a very beautiful modern[4] design and should give its owner considerable pride and satisfaction during a lifetime of usefulness.[6]

When you are ready to make your selection of pieces, we should like to be of service to you in planning your[8] set and in marking your silver. We have a staff of skilled designers who are ready to submit sketches of[10] engraving for your approval as soon as you write us what initials you wish to use.

Very sincerely yours,   (115)

100

Mrs. Ronald Hays
55 West 14 Street
Grand Rapids, Michigan

Dear Mrs. Hays:

The January sales now being held throughout the store offer exceptional values in every department.[2]

As an added convenience for you, we have opened a charge account, eliminating all formalities.[4] Your signature alone is required as a matter of record.

There is a new spirit of youthfulness throughout[6] our store—complete stocks from which to make your selections and courteous, competent salespeople to serve you promptly[8] and satisfactorily.

And behind it all is a reputation of almost a hundred years for honest[10] merchandise, high quality and prices that are always moderate.

We are anxious to have your patronage, and[12] if you will return the enclosed card, your account may be used at any time.

Cordially yours,   (134)

101

Mrs. L. Mogul
15 West 13 Street
Boise, Idaho

My dear Friend:

Will you be free to spend the summer with us? I should be most happy to have you. The children and their mother, as[2] well as I, wish you would feel that our home is always open to you. Our garden is beautiful now, and my[4] brother said just last night how much good he thought a few days in the country would do you. Be sure and come to us if you[6] can. Rest assured we will do our best to make you have a good time.

Faithfully yours,   (71)

102

Mr. George A. Stockholm
Bentley High School
Danbury, Connecticut

Dear Mr. Stockholm:

One of the outstanding features of Modern Dictation is the shorthand vocabulary in each lesson. This[2] word list enables the pupil to prepare his assignments with the assurance that he is practicing correct[4] outlines for unfamiliar words.

Modern Dictation should be placed in the hands of every advanced pupil[6] and used for daily homework and classroom drill. It will increase the efficiency of your commercial department[8] by helping you to develop even more shorthand writers of the highest type. The progressive shorthand teacher[10] of today is looking for just such a book.

If you will mail your order now, you will begin the Fall term with the[12] feeling that your dictation troubles are over.

Very cordially yours,   (129)

103

Mrs. Stanley M. Gordon
317 Westover Avenue
Trenton, New Jersey

Dear Madam:

Men and women frequently ask us what it costs to keep the Arctic in good condition. There is no service charge,[2] because the Arctic requires no service. Every part of the cooling unit is permanently sealed against[4] the wear and tear of time and rust. There are neither belts nor pulleys to give trouble.

Great effort has been made to supply[6] you with an electric refrigerator that will be a constant reminder of its convenience. Every[8] possible cause of trouble has been eliminated. The Arctic never needs oiling because the original[10] oil stays fresh and pure forever.

The Arctic is a woman's refrigerator and is built to offer[12] her the most efficient service.

Very truly yours,   (126)

104

Mr. Arthur Goodman
134 River Road
Montgomery, Alabama
Dear Sir:

The banquet took place last night. We all enjoyed seeing the hockey leader from your town. In the evening we went to[2] the rink and watched a game between two classes of college students. It was a fast game and very interesting. We[4] were all shocked at seeing one of the players hurt. We fear he will be crippled for life, as one leg is badly shattered.[6]

Sincerely yours,   (60)

105

Mrs. Muriel Abel
75 Ocean Avenue
Brooklyn 30, New York
My dear Friend:

We have been looking for a letter from you for a long time. If you would write to us oftener, you would get more[2] good out of your work. In this way you would then be putting it to use just as fast as you went along.

When we get[4] a letter and a paper from you, the first thing we do is to mark your paper and then we read your letter. In[6] this way we find out just what you are doing, and in our answer we can speak to you just as though you were here in[8] person. We hope to hear from you soon.

Sincerely yours,   (86)

106

Quality Offset Company
23 Broad Street
Houston, Texas
Gentlemen:

On May first we sent you an order for three new pass-books to be used in our small country store in Springfield. Up to[2] the present we have had no word from you. It is possible that the letter was lost, but we should like to know at[4] once if you can take the order.

We have changed our plans about putting in the new pass-books in the city store. We[6] believe that because so many people have used the others they will not wish to buy the new. Maybe later on we[8] shall be willing to do as your order man writes.

However, just now we do not wish to change, and we are sure you[10] will understand.

We shall have our fall order ready for you as soon as we get word from our buyer. He will be[12] here by the end of the week, and we shall write you at once.

Very truly yours,   (130)

107

Mr. George A. Stockholm
Bentley High School
Danbury, Connecticut
Dear Mr. Stockholm:

Does your present dictation book have in each lesson a shorthand word list that is easily available to[2] the pupil? Modern Dictation does.

Are the words in your book counted in groups that make it easy to dictate at any[4] desired speed? Are the letters and articles graded according to difficulty? Are they arranged in[6] progressive order? In Modern Dictation they are.

Is the type in your book kind to the eye? Is the paper free from[8] glare? Is the content based on good business English and actual business knowledge? Modern Dictation has all of[10] these desirable features.

Give your classes a real treat by ordering your supply of Modern Dictation now.[12]

Very cordially yours,   (120)

108

Superior Shoe Company
Superior Building
Manchester, New Hampshire
Gentlemen:

This morning we received twelve cases of shoes which we are sorry you shipped at this particular time. We explained[2] to your salesman that we did not want the shoes before August 1 because we have our annual sale during July[4] and have no available storeroom now.

We had decided to discontinue another line of shoes and[6] were planning to give you this extra business. If your policy requires early shipments, it would be a mistake[8] for us to make a change.

We do not know whether your shipping department or your salesman made the mistake in[10] forwarding this shipment. We are decidedly disappointed because your representative assured us that you[12] would give us full cooperation.

Yours very truly,   (126)

109

Dr. Harry U. Powers
Superintendent of Schools
Hamilton, Pennsylvania

Dear Dr. Powers:

We were indeed glad to learn from your letter of January 18 that your school board is[2] again considering the organization of a driver training program.

We are happy to give you[4] permission to use any of our materials for local publicity to support your efforts. We should,[6] furthermore, be glad to send you cuts of charts and drawings that show the need for teaching our high school boys and girls[8] how to drive safely. Will you please examine our booklets and then let us know what will help you?

Very cordially yours,   (101)

110

Mr. Frank C. Johnson
1341 South Boulevard
Baltimore, Maryland
Dear Mr. Johnson:

Your letter of June 15 was received and has had our careful consideration.

At first, we thought we might be[2] able to send you one or two letters to assist in the excellent work that you are doing. Our policy,[4] however, has been decidedly against permitting any material of that nature to leave our files. We[6] should, therefore, prefer not to make any exception, even though you intend to make the best possible use of the[8] letters.

We are writing this so that you may know we did not simply throw your letter away but gave it thoughtful[10] attention. We regret that, under the circumstances, we can not make a favorable reply to your[12] request.

Very cordially yours, (121)

111

Mrs. Stanley M. Gordon
317 Westover Avenue
Trenton, New Jersey
Dear Madam:

In these modern days there is little need of our trying to tell you the advantages or pleasures to be gained[2] by equipping your home with an electric refrigerator. There is, however, a very definite reason[4] for our inviting you to see the new Arctic. We want you on our list of customers.

Your judgment tells you that[6] any electric refrigerator has many good features that make it both practical and economical. The[8] Arctic is also a beautiful piece of furniture that will fit easily into any kitchen plan.

Visit[10] our display rooms and let us show you the various sizes. The simple beauty of the Arctic is always[12] in style.

Very truly yours, (121)

112

Mr. George A. Stockholm
Bentley High School
Danbury, Connecticut

Dear Mr. Stockholm:

It has been a pleasure to send you, with our compliments, a copy of Modern Dictation. This is the very[2] latest textbook for the advanced shorthand class. We are sure that you will want to give it careful study.

Part I is[4] devoted entirely to letters that have appeared in state examinations during the past few years. Part[6] II will meet with the full approval of every teacher of dictation. It contains a wealth of letter[8] material dealing with various types of business. Part III includes an excellent selection of short articles[10] and speeches chosen for their value in furnishing information about business and office routine.

Why[12] not write us your opinion of this book?

Very cordially yours,   (127)

113

John W. Evans Company
8 Main Street
Garden City, New York

Gentlemen:

We were glad to receive your fine order and to learn from your letter of May 22 how Walker fishing equipment has increased your volume of sales.

We have proved many times that our national advertising[4] does bring business to our dealers. Our colorful window and counter displays have also been very successful[6] in promoting sales.

The new edition of our pocket-sized catalog, A HANDBOOK FOR FISHERMEN, will be[8] ready in a few weeks. Please let us know how many you will want for your customers.

Yours truly,   (93)

114

Mrs. Stanley M. Gordon
317 Westover Avenue
Trenton, New Jersey
Dear Madam:

A lady recently told one of our salesmen that her kitchen was so small that it would not accommodate the[2] big electric refrigerators displayed in the local stores. Now she owns an Arctic.

The Arctic has two[4] valuable features when size is considered. The large flat top is easy to reach, easy to clean, and convenient[6] to use. It does away with the necessity of a kitchen table. In spite of the low top, however, the Arctic[8] cabinet is high enough to permit easy floor cleaning.

We wish you could find the time to see this refrigerator[10] that has added so much happiness to so many happy homes.

Very truly yours   (113)

115

Mrs. Stanley M. Gordon
317 Westover Avenue
Trenton, New Jersey
Dear Madam:

Among the many outstanding advantages of the Arctic is an electric light that is built into the[2] cabinet and operates automatically when the door is opened. This is how it works. As you gently[4] press the door latch, the door swings open and the light comes on, bringing the whole interior into clear view.

See[6] how conveniently arranged the refrigerator is! Observe that the shelves are made so that even small[8] containers will not upset.

The box is easily cleaned because the white enamel is guaranteed to be stainless.[10] There are no sharp corners and the smooth edges will aid you in keeping the box sanitary.

Why not come in soon[12] for a complete demonstration?

Very truly yours,   (126)

116

Mr. George A. Stockholm
Bentley High School
Danbury, Connecticut

Dear Mr. Stockholm:

We have not heard from you and we are wondering whether you received the copy of Modern Dictation that you[2] requested several weeks ago. Please drop us a line if you did not receive it.

If you did receive your copy,[4] we hope that you have had a chance to give it a most careful examination. The preface explains the[6] purpose underlying the planning of each division and makes some excellent suggestions for the successful[8] use of the book.

We are so eager to have you try Modern Dictation in your classes that we are offering[10] you a liberal allowance on your old books. This exchange does not affect the usual school discount.

Very cordially yours,   (119)

117

Mrs. Stanley M. Gordon
317 Westover Avenue
Trenton, New Jersey

Dear Madam:

We do not want to bore you with our letters about the Arctic refrigerator. We did hope that they would cause[2] you to visit our display rooms for a complete demonstration. When you know the Arctic as we do, you will surely[4] appreciate its many excellent points.

If one is considering cost, the Arctic has a special[6] appeal. The new cooling system and the modern cabinet make possible the greatest operating economy.[8]

It is so easy to buy the Arctic. Our budget plan places it within the reach of everyone. A[10] few dollars a month will provide kitchen happiness that you can never realize until you possess an Arctic.[12]

Very truly yours,   (120)

119

Mr. Edward R. Smith
Board of Education
12 State Street
Harrisburg 10, Pennsylvania

Dear Mr. Smith:

In response to your request of March 2, we are glad to add your name to the mailing list of our[2] monthly publication, FLOOR LIFE.

Your interest in our magazine indicates to us that you realize proper[4] maintenance of floors is a serious matter at this time. Each issue will help you because you will benefit[6] from the experience of others who are facing the same problems.

You know that our factories are pledged to[8] fast production of new products, but you also know we are prepared to help in essential maintenance work.

Please[10] let us know if there is any way in which we may be of service to you.

Very sincerely yours,   (117)

120

Mr. Edward R. Smith
Board of Education
12 State Street
Harrisburg 10, Pennsylvania

Dear Mr. Smith:

Since we wrote you on March 5, you have received the March and April issue of FLOOR LIFE. You have had[2] an opportunity to become acquainted with our bulletin and we should like to have your suggestions for[4] its improvement. We should also be glad to have you send in some material from your own experience for[6] the June issue.

We are both interested in floor maintenance because we know that proper care pays in four ways.[8] First, it keeps floors in good condition. Second, it promotes health. Third, it prevents accidents. Fourth, it saves money.

Our[10] new catalogue, which has been mailed to you, will help you with current problems and with your future plans.

Very truly yours, (120)

121

Wilson Chemical Corporation
325 Broadway
New York 7, New York
Gentlemen:

After reading your material on floor maintenance, I can see that some building superintendents[2] have problems more difficult than mine.

Our Wilson equipment was purchased in 19 and has been in[4] constant use. These sanding, scrubbing, and polishing machines have been very satisfactory and we are proud of[6] the condition of our floors. Long years of steady service, however, will probably make it necessary for[8] some of these machines to be repaired before the heavy demands of the school vacation period can be met.[10]

Will you arrange for an inspection of our equipment some time this month in order that we may know which machines[12] must be repaired before July 1?

Very truly yours, (130)

122

Mr. Edward R. Smith
Board of Education
12 State Street
Harrisburg 10, Pennsylvania
Dear Mr. Smith:

Thank you for your letter of April 12. We have asked our factory representative in Baltimore,[2] Mr. Fred Bradley, to take care of your equipment as soon as possible.

Although our force of trained men[4] is being increased as rapidly as possible, we are still unable to meet the demands as promptly as[6] we should like. We know you will be patient about any delay, since all our men have crowded schedules. You may feel[8] certain, however, that we are doing everything in our power to give good service.

We are glad your Wilson[10] floor machines have given satisfaction for so many years because our reputation is built upon the[12] quality of our products and the praise of satisfied customers.

Very sincerely yours,   (136)

123

Wilson Chemical Corporation
325 Broadway
New York 7, New York
Gentlemen:

Mr. Bradley's inspection of our floor equipment was very helpful. We were pleasantly surprised[2] to learn that only two machines will have to be sent to your factory in Rockford for rebuilding. They will be[4] shipped immediately and we shall expect you to check on this job frequently to avoid any delay.

The[6] other necessary repairs fortunately can be made here. Mr. Bradley has promised to be in Harrisburg[8] with a mechanic during the week of May 21 to take care of this work.

We shall be able to start[10] our heavy schedule of vacation work on time if our floor machines are returned promptly. Your cooperation[12] in this regard will be appreciated.

Very truly yours,   (131)

124

Mr. Edward R. Smith
Board of Education
12 State Street
Harrisburg 10, Pennsylvania
Dear Mr. Smith:
 We were glad to learn from your letter of May 2 that your Wilson floor equipment is in such good[2] condition.
 We shall keep in touch with the two machines in Rockford and we can see no reason now why they should not[4] be back in Harrisburg early in June.
 Mr. Bradley reports that later this month he is going to refinish[6] one of your gymnasium floors with our SPORT-FLOOR SEAL. You will then be able to compare our product with the[8] one you are now using and this is a test we welcome. We know you will be convinced that SPORTFLOOR SEAL is the solution[10] of your gymnasium floor problem.

Very sincerely yours,   (112)

125

Mrs. Ronald Duncan
17 Ocean Avenue
Brooklyn 13, New York
My dear Mrs. Duncan:
 Would you enjoy living in a residential park of over 500 acres of high, healthy, beautifully[2] wooded, fertile land on Long Island and yet be within 18 minutes from New York via the Pennsylvania[4] Railroad with trains going to and fro every ten minutes or so—electric lights, gas, sewers, cement walks[6] and telephones all installed?
 Thirty-five minutes from New York on the same railroad I have other delightful places[8] for homes and home sites. I would appreciate a line from you, so that if interested I may tell you more[10] of both places. The properties are most valuable as an investment as well as a home.

Very truly yours,   (117)

126

The Bowman Gift Shop
78 Elm Street
Syracuse 3, New York
Gentlemen:

Orders for our Christmas packages of writing paper have been coming in steadily since our[2] illustrated booklet was mailed early in August.

When we completed our plans for holiday stationery, we[4] felt certain that our customers would be pleased. The large number of orders and the enthusiastic comments of[6] our dealers have convinced us that this holiday assortment is the most popular we have ever offered.

This[8] paper comes packed in beautiful Christmas boxes and also in boxes with removable holiday wrappers.[10] This makes it possible for you not only to take advantage of our low prices but also to dispose of[12] your surplus stock after the holidays.

May we have your order within a few days?

Yours truly,   (137)

127

New England Paper Company
33 Ware Avenue
Worcester 5, Massachusetts
Gentlemen:

Our order for holiday writing paper has not been placed because we still have a large stock on hand.[2] You will recall that the order we sent you on May 2 did not reach us until July 7. Our summer sales were[4] greatly reduced by the delay in the delivery of this order.

We like your special offer and realize[6] the value of displaying stationery in attractive holiday packages. We are unable at[8] this time to place our usual Christmas order because we cannot afford to carry over our old stock until[10] next spring.

We should like to have a fresh stock for our spring and summer business. Have you any suggestions for[12] solving our problem?

Very truly yours,   (127)

128

The Bowman Gift Shop
78 Elm Street
Syracuse 3, New York
Gentlemen:

We regret that the late delivery of your spring order has upset your plans for your holiday[2] stationery business.

In our letter of May 23 we explained that the situation was caused by[4] forces beyond our control and we therefore granted you a special discount. Now let us cooperate again.[6]

We shall be glad to send you attractive holiday wrappers for your present stock if you will send us on November[8] 26 an inventory of our stationery in your store. Simply list the stock number and the quantity[10] on hand. You will then be in a position to dispose of this paper during the Christmas season.

We[12] can also make prompt delivery of your other holiday needs.

Yours truly   (134)

129

New England Paper Company
33 Ware Avenue
Worcester 5, Massachusetts
Gentlemen:

Thank you for your generous offer of September 27, which seems to solve our problem. We[2] shall send you on November 26 the information requested concerning the required number of holiday[4] wrappers.

We should like to place a definite order for additional holiday goods at this time in[6] order to obtain the advantages of your special offer. However, it is impossible for us to[8] do so until we know what the condition of our stock will be later in the fall.

We are therefore enclosing[10] a tentative order which may be changed ōn or about November 18. Please reserve this stationery so[12] that we may take advantage of your holiday offer if our present stock sells rapidly enough.

Very truly[14] yours. (141)

130

The Bowman Gift Shop
78 Elm Street
Syracuse 3, New York
Gentlemen:

The tentative order which you enclosed in your letter of October 3 will enable you to[2] receive the advantages of our special holiday offer. We gladly make this exception because we feel[4] that we are responsible for your unusual stock problem.

Your attention is called to the enclosed folder[6] which explains in detail a new type of service that we shall offer our dealers after January 1. We[8] shall then be equipped to give prompt service on orders for printed and engraved stationery at very reasonable[10] rates. Our high quality paper with fine printing or engraving rates increase your business.

Read this folder[12] carefully and then make an early resolution to start the New Year right.

Yours truly, (136)

131

New England Paper Company
33 Ware Avenue
Worcester 5, Massachusetts
Gentlemen:

We find it necessary to reduce the tentative order which we sent you on October 3.[2] Our stock of Delta No. 9 and Persian

No. 8 is adequate for the present. Therefore, please fill our order[4] with the exception of these two items. Please ship these goods not later than November 30.

For several[6] years our orders for printed stationery have been satisfactorily handled by a local printer. There[8] is, however, a demand for high-grade engraved stationery. Send us the display outfit and we will give the matter[10] our attention.

In this connection you realize that from the dealer's point of view, a low retail price, a[12] fair profit, and prompt delivery are the important factors.

Very truly yours,   (135)

132

Mr. James L. Archer
32 Central Avenue
Rome, New York
Dear Mr. Archer:
We are glad to know that you are interested in our products and we have asked the Central[2] Hardware Company to mail you a copy of our catalog.

Experience has proved to us that we can give[4] better service to our many friends by having a complete stock of fishing tackle ready for inspection[6] near their homes.

The sporting goods department of the Central Hardware Company has been a meeting place for fishermen[8] for many years. Won't you visit this friendly store at 275 South Street and look over the latest ideas[10] in fishing equipment?

The reputation of this reliable store and our guarantee are back of every[12] Walker product.

Yours very truly,   (125)

133

Empire Roofing Corporation
79 Park Street
Dayton 8, Ohio
Gentlemen:

If satisfactory arrangements can be made, we should like to add Empire roofing materials[2] to our line of building supplies.

Our wide experience over a period of 22 years in Westchester[4] County places us in a position to bring your products to the attention of the best building contractors.[6] Our volume of business entitles us, we believe, to an appointment as the exclusive distributor[8] for this county. Perhaps it would be wise to have a representative come to White Plains to discuss this[10] proposition.

Please give this matter your prompt attention and let us hear from you soon because we are making very[12] definite plans for the future expansion in building.

Very truly yours,   (133)

134

Eastern Supply Company
24 King Street
White Plains, New York
Gentlemen:

We appreciate your letter of September 20 and we are glad to learn that you are interested[2] in becoming the distributor of our roofing materials in Westchester County.

Your suggestion[4] that we send a representative to discuss this matter is a good one. One of our best qualified men,[6] Mr. Charles E. Atwood, will telephone you from New York within a few days to arrange an appointment. He has[8] spent years in sales promotion work and we are confident that you will find his advice very helpful. We shall eagerly[10] await the report of this conference.

It is always a pleasure to learn that people in the building[12] industry have such a high regard for Empire roofing.

Very truly yours,   (133)

135

Eastern Supply Company
24 King Street
White Plains, New York
Gentlemen:

Mr. Atwood was in the office yesterday to tell us about his visit with you on September[2] 29.

We discussed the entire matter with him and considered very carefully the memorandum[4] that he left you. We believe this provides the basis for friendly business relations and we are, therefore,[6] enclosing a contract for your consideration. After reading this contract, you will see that we have followed[8] the points covered in your talk with Mr. Atwood.

The reputation of Empire products has been built on high quality[10] and fair dealings at all times. You may be sure that we are sincerely interested in having you join[12] our family of distributors.

Very truly yours,   (130)

136

Empire Roofing Corporation
79 Park Street
Dayton 8, Ohio
Gentlemen:

Thank you for your letter of October 7.

The contract is very satisfactory and we[2] are glad to enclose one copy, which has been properly signed.

As men become available, we plan to develop[4] a sales force that will reach the consumer directly. We do not intend to go into the contracting business,[6] of course, but we do intend to build a trained sales force that will appreciate the advantages that will[8] come from a trained sales force, a fine display room, and a large stock.

We shall be glad to have the benefit of your advice[10] at any time.

Very truly yours,   (107)

137

Eastern Supply Company
24 King Street
White Plains, New York
Gentlemen:

It is a pleasure to learn from your letter of October 13 that you have decided to distribute[2] Empire roofing materials.

Your plans for a trained sales force and a display room indicate clearly that[4] you are going to obtain a large volume of business in future building.

Under separate cover we[6] are sending you a copy of PLANNING AND ORGANIZING A CONSUMER SALES FORCE. This confidential loose-leaf[8] notebook contains many ideas that come from the practical and successful experience of hundreds of[10] our distributors.

We are glad to be able to send you the book, since it points the way to more business and[12] larger profits.

Very truly yours,   (126)

138

Eastern Supply Company
24 King Street
White Plains, New York
Gentlemen:

Will you let us know if you have any questions as the result of your study of our notebook, PLANNING[2] AND ORGANIZING A CONSUMER SALES FORCE?

Your future planning should include an attractive time-payment plan[4] to enable your seven salesmen to increase business. If you have any difficulty in working out[6] a plan locally, we shall be glad to give you suggestions from the experience of other distributors.[8]

The need for protecting existing buildings in these days of limited construction means that there is much roofing[10] business at the present time. Materials are available for necessary maintenance and repairs.[12] We suggest, therefore, that you let Empire products start earning profits for you now.

Very truly yours   (137)

139

Western Hardware Corporation
92 Seneca Street
Pittsburgh 2, Pennsylvania
Gentlemen:

In a few days you will receive our new catalogue of hand tools.

The purpose of this catalogue is[2] to provide our dealers with a complete list of hand tools and supplies for which there is a steady demand. The clear[4] explanations and descriptions will make it easy for you to make your selections.

From experience you know[6] that Medlock tools are designed and built for skilled workmen. For more than sixty years our firm has been a recognized source[8] of supply for dependable tools.

We advise that you let us take care of your needs now while our stock is complete,[10] because no one knows what the demand will be in a few months.

Very truly yours,   (114)

140

Western Hardware Corporation
92 Seneca Street
Pittsburgh 2, Pennsylvania
Gentlemen:

We are writing to urge that you permit us to fill your hand tool order while we are in a position[2] to do so promptly.

Since we sent you our new catalogue in August, the demands upon the manufacturers[4] of hand tools have greatly increased. We have increased the production capacity of our factory in an[6] effort to cooperate fully with the increasing needs of our customers. We are, at the same time, doing[8] our best to supply our dealers all over the country with the same high-quality hand tools that have made the name[10] of Medlock famous.

We can assure you that there will be no price changes before November 1. Your order can be[12] handled promptly now.

Yours very truly,   (127)

141

The Medlock Tool Company
55 Harrison Avenue
Bridgeport 8, Connecticut
Gentlemen:

We are enclosing two purchase orders for tools and supplies.

Please note carefully that the items listed[2] on purchase order No. 5280 are to be shipped by express directly to the Bates Vocational[4] School on Crown Street in this city.

Prompt handling of this school order is very important to us. The large[6] increase in registration in the shop courses this fall has resulted in an urgent need for this equipment at once. Although we have been seeking the business of this school for several years, this is the first contract that has[10] been given to our company.

It is, therefore, to our advantage to show them that our service really is[12] superior.

Yours truly,   (125)

142

Western Hardware Corporation
92 Seneca Street
Pittsburgh 2, Pennsylvania
Gentlemen:

Thank you for your letter of October 10 in which you enclosed two purchase orders. We appreciate[2] this business and are glad that you have given us the opportunity to supply your needs for this fall[4] before any adjustments in prices are necessary.

The manager of our shipping department has received[6] orders to rush the Bates Vocational School order. You may feel certain that this equipment will reach the school[8] without delay. We are just as eager as you are to maintain your reputation for superior service.[10]

The rapid growth of industrial courses in large cities during the past few years means increased tool business.[12] Here is a good opportunity for increased sales and real service.

Yours very truly,   (136)

143

Western Hardware Corporation
92 Seneca Street
Pittsburgh 2, Pennsylvania
Gentlemen:

This morning we received a request to submit a bid on the equipment specifications for[2] the new vocational school now being erected in Erie, Pa.

It is our policy, as[4] you know, to work only through our regular dealers. Therefore, we suggest that you send a representative to[6] follow up this opportunity for some very good business.

We can be very helpful to you in preparing[8] your estimate on the list of hand tools, and we hope you will let us work with you. The large machine equipment,[10] of course, is out of our line. Because of your long experience in this field, we know you will have no trouble[12] in submitting a complete bill.

Yours very truly,   (129)

144

The Medlock Tool Company
55 Harrison Avenue
Bridgeport 8, Connecticut
Gentlemen:

We appreciate the information that you gave us in your letter of October 17.[2]

The purchasing agent for the Board of Education in Erie has given us permission to submit a[4] bid on the equipment list for the new school. Since the bid must be submitted on or before November 19,[6] it is necessary for us to work rapidly.

Some time ago you stated that there might be price changes after[8] November 1. While we understand that increasing demands are being placed on the tool industry, still, we[10] must request a definite guarantee from your company that the prices in effect now will apply to the[12] Erie school contract if it is awarded to our company.

Yours truly,   (133)

145

Shaw Hardware Company
89 John Street
Watertown, New York
Gentlemen:

Our records show that just one year ago today your first order reached our office. We are happy to[2] greet you on this business birthday and to express our appreciation of your orders.

This year of pleasant[4] business relations will, we sincerely hope, lead to many years of profitable business friendship.

We[6] realize, of course, that the goodwill of our old friends and the confidence of our new customers depend directly[8] on our merchandise and the quality of our service. Therefore, we are eager to have your frank opinion.[10] Will you please use the enclosed questionnaire and addressed envelope to let us know how we may be of greater service[12] to you?

Very truly yours,   (125)

146

Allen & White, Inc.
25 Fulton Street
New York 2, New York
Gentlemen:

The questionnaire which you sent us on April 3 is enclosed. We have checked this form carefully and hope[2] it will prove helpful to you.

We should like in particular to call your attention to the inconvenience[4] that your credit terms have caused us. Naturally we are proud that we have always been able to discount our invoices.[6] During the past year, however, it has been difficult at times to arrange payment of your bills before[8] the tenth of the following month to earn the 2 per cent discount.

Since much of our business is rural, our[10] collections are frequently slow. It is, therefore, important for us to buy where our credit rating will obtain a[12] longer discount period.

Yours very truly,   (128)

147

Mr. William E. Shaw
Shaw Hardware Company
89 John Street
Watertown, New York
Dear Mr. Shaw:

Thank you for the prompt attention given to our questionnaire. We also appreciate your letter[2] of April 8 because it gives us an opportunity to study your problem. We want you to feel that[4] this company is always interested in the success of your business.

We have, therefore, directed Mr.[6] James King of our credit department to discuss terms of payment with you.

Mr. King will attend a convention[8] of credit managers in Syracuse from May 2 to May 4. If it is convenient for you, he can[10] discuss your problem with you either before or after this meeting.

Mr. King will telephone you next week to[12] set a date for his visit to your store.

Very sincerely yours,   (131)

148

Mr. William E. Shaw
Shaw Hardware Company
89 John Street
Watertown, New York

Dear Mr. Shaw:

Thank you for your courtesy to Mr. King, who reports that he had a very satisfactory[2] discussion with you on May 5.

Mr. King believes that he understands your problem and that you realize[4] how important it is for us to maintain a uniform credit policy.

Whenever it seems necessary,[6] as Mr. King pointed out to you, we shall be glad to consider a request for an extension of the[8] discount period to enable you to meet an unusual situation.

Mr. King was favorably[10] impressed by your modern store with its complete stock. Our high quality products, of course, belong in your type of[12] store. We assure you, therefore, of our sincere desire to cooperate.

Very sincerely yours, (137)

149

Allen & White, Inc.
25 Fulton Street
New York 2, New York

Gentlemen:

In your letter of May 8, you indicated a desire to cooperate when an unusual[2] credit situation developed. We are now faced with a credit problem.

On July 7, Mr. Williams[4] displayed your fall line of sporting goods. Since we have built up a good business in sporting goods in this section,[6] we should like to arrange for our fall stock now. However, it would be a hardship for us to order and be forced[8] to pay by August 10 to earn the 2 per cent discount.

Since our income from this merchandise will not begin until[10] after schools open in September, we will not place our order unless an extension of the discount period[12] is granted.

Yours very truly, (127)

150

Mr. William E. Shaw
Shaw Hardware Company
89 John Street
Watertown, New York
Dear Mr. Shaw:

We are glad that you did not hesitate to write us concerning the credit problem in connection² with your fall order for sporting goods.

Because of your excellent credit rating and the volume of business⁴ which you have given us, we shall be happy to accept your order now and date the invoice September 1.⁶ This arrangement will extend the discount period to October 10.

It is sound business to save by taking⁸ advantage of discounts. We realize how you feel because we make every effort to plan our collections¹⁰ so that we also may discount our invoices. We are able, as a result, to offer our high quality¹² products at very attractive prices.

                                        Very sincerely yours,   (131)

151

The Royal Laundry, Inc.
82 Palmer Street
Buffalo 6, New York
Gentlemen:

Good health is vital to a community and good laundry service is vital to the health of every² city.

Since you have an obligation to your city, we feel that it is our duty to make your Johnson⁴ equipment work better and last longer. Regular inspections, as shown in the booklet you received a few weeks ago, will prevent breakdowns. Repairs to machinery mean lost time and the waste of valuable materials.⁸

You can protect your equipment by using one of our SERVICE PLANS in your plant. Your present equipment¹⁰ is priceless. It deserves the attention that our service plans provide. Only Johnson experts can give the service¹² you need.

Won't you give this important problem careful thought?
                                        Yours truly,   (132)

152

Johnson Manufacturing Company
31 William Street
Hartford 4, Connecticut
Gentlemen:

Our engineer has studied your service plans and his report was received this morning.

Since most of our[2] equipment is less than four years old, he states that the cost of this special service would not be justified. We realize[4] the importance of keeping our machines in the best possible condition. Our engineer, however,[6] believes that all ordinary service jobs can be handled by our own men. We have some very capable mechanics[8] who have been with our company for years. We hope that they will be able to remain with us.

We assume[10] that your usual emergency service will be available. Later on we may find it advisable[12] to use one of your special services.

Very truly yours,   (130)

153

The Royal Laundry, Inc.
82 Palmer Street
Buffalo 6, New York
Gentlemen:

Thank you for your letter of November 17.

You are, of course, in a very strong position[2] today because you have kept your plant modern by buying new equipment regularly.

This new equipment, however,[4] will be carrying a much heavier load than it has in the past, because of the large increase in your[6] business. Since replacement parts are expensive and their installation time-consuming, every effort should[8] be made to avoid any breakdown that will require new parts.

We honestly believe that you need our factory-trained[10] experts to help your men keep your laundry equipment in good working order.

Emergency service will be[12] given whenever possible. One of our SERVICE PLANS, however, will reduce your need for emergency service.[14]

Yours truly,   (142)

154

Johnson Manufacturing Company
31 William Street
Hartford 4, Connecticut
Gentlemen:

We have just sent you a telegram concerning the trouble that has developed in our rotary[2] dryer. A copy of this telegram is enclosed. We expect that our call will receive prompt attention because[4] you know how important this dryer is in our business.

As a result of this emergency, we have again[6] discussed your service plans with our engineer. We have decided to put your limited SERVICE PLAN in[8] operation because of transportation difficulties and material shortages. This plan will provide a[10] complete semi-annual inspection of our machines.

Please arrange to have this SERVICE PLAN start at once so that[12] we may have the first inspection very soon.

Very truly yours,   (131)

155

The Royal Laundry, Inc.
82 Palmer Street
Buffalo 6, New York
Gentlemen:

When we received your telegram on December 8, we immediately telephoned our Mr.[2] Wilson, who was in Rochester. We are glad that we had such a capable man so near Buffalo when your trouble developed. Without doubt he has your machine back in service by this time.

Your request for the limited SERVICE[6] PLAN will be given prompt attention. Our experts will be at your plant for the first inspection as soon as arrangements[8] can be made.

Since our staff of trained men has so many demands made upon it, you will understand that trips must[10] be carefully planned. In this way, a small number of trained men can give excellent service at regular intervals[12] to many plants.

Yours truly,   (130·)

156

Charles A. Black & Company
77 Pine Street
Buffalo 7, New York
Gentlemen:

This morning we received a very pleasing report from Mr. George Johnson, our representative[2] in western New York.

At his request we have sent you one case of sample boxes of our white Wellington blackboard[4] chalk. We suggest that you ask your school customers to give this chalk a trial in the classroom. We are confident[6] of the result of this trial because we know that Wellington is a pure, dustless chalk that produces a clear,[8] white line. This experiment will convince your customers that Wellington chalk is superior.

Long experience[10] has shown that Wellington chalk is the most economical for school use. It lasts longer and contains no[12] material which will harm blackboards.

Very truly yours,   (129)

157

Charles A. Black & Company
77 Pine Street
Buffalo 7, New York
Gentlemen:

About one month ago we sent you a case of our white Wellington blackboard chalk for trial use. We[2] shall be much interested in the reports you receive from these trials.

Your customers will find that Wellington[4] makes a soft, smooth, legible line and is absolutely dustless. It is guaranteed to outlast ordinary[6] chalks. The pure materials in Wellington chalk and its uniform quality keep blackboards in fine writing condition.[8]

A school supply house of your standing naturally wants to stock the finest chalk. We believe that we make that[10] chalk.

A price list is enclosed for your convenience. Please let us know if there is anything we can do to help[12] you.

Very truly yours, (124)

158

The Wellington Chalk Company
32 Fourth Avenue
New York 4, New York

Gentlemen:

Please give your prompt attention to the enclosed purchase order.

The school trials which you suggested have[2] brought in some very favorable responses. We have, therefore, decided to list your Wellington chalk in our[4] next catalogue. You can help by sending us suitable copy and suggestions for our printer.

Since 80 per cent[6] of our school orders come in between May 15 and the opening of schools in September, it is important[8] that we have complete information for our new catalogue by November 27. This catalogue[10] goes to press on December 1.

Do you manufacture Wellington chalk in colors? We have a steady demand[12] for a good colored chalk for blackboard use.

Very truly yours, (130)

159

Charles A. Black & Company
77 Pine Street
Buffalo 7, New York
Gentlemen:

Thank you for your letter of November 9. We are always pleased to learn that the high quality of[2] our products has been recognized.

You will be glad to know that a Wellington colored chalk is now ready for the[4] market. For several years we have worked to overcome the weaknesses so often found' in colored chalks. The new[6] product has rich, bright colors and the strength of our white chalk. A supply of samples has been sent to you.

Please read the[8] story of the development of this chalk in the enclosed booklet, Brightening the Classroom with Wellington.[10]

Material for your catalogue will be prepared and mailed to you within a few days.

Very truly yours,   (119)

160

The Wellington Chalk Company
32 Fourth Avenue
New York 4, New York
Gentlemen:

We appreciate your cooperation in sending us the material for listing Wellington[2] chalk in our new catalogue. The selection of cuts will help our printer.

Our catalogue is always issued[4] early in January so that we may be ready for the extra school orders that are placed for the second[6] term. But, as you know, most large school orders come in the summer rush.

We assume that all large orders will be shipped direct[8] to our customers. This will mean a real saving for us.

Since we have had a few inquiries, we note with interest[10] in the folder you sent us that you manufacture a special sight-saving chalk in golden color.[12]

Very truly yours,   (123)

161

Charles A. Black & Company
77 Pine Street
Buffalo 7 New York
Gentlemen:

Thank you for your letter of November 22. We have sent you samples of our special sight-saving[2] chalk. We are also glad to inform you that direct shipment will be made to any address on orders for[4] ten or more cases. Transportation charges will be prepaid and charged to your account.

We have a suggestion for[6] your dull season. Your location should make our chalks for industrial use an excellent addition to your stock.[8] There is always a regular demand for the special chalks described in the enclosed folder.

This matter deserves[10] careful consideration. When our Mr. Johnson calls early in December, why not let him help you develop[12] this profitable field?

Very truly yours,   (128)

162

Randall and Peck, Inc.
35 Draper Avenue
Rochester 10, New York
Gentlemen:

The enclosed booklet, Make Your Own Weather, will show you how to maintain your volume of business through[2] the hot months.

Read about our new Scott portable room cooler that will bring summer comfort to homes, offices, hospitals[4] and hotels in your city. It is an air-conditioning unit that is quiet and beautiful. It[6] is almost as easy to install as a radio. It can be moved from room to room and from building to building.[8] You cannot afford to overlook this opportunity.

To help our dealers, we have arranged a demonstration[10] at the factory on April 8 and 9. We invite your sales and service managers to attend this[12] meeting at our expense.

Very truly yours,   (127)

163

The Scott Company
93 Carpenter Street
Springfield 7, Massachusetts
Gentlemen:

Our sales manager, **Mr. William Blake,** and a representative from our service department will[2] attend your demonstration on April 8 and 9. We appreciate your cooperation in providing[4] this opportunity for our men to become acquainted with your new cooling units.

We have, as you know, installed[6] 28 of your combination heating and air-conditioning systems. The new portable unit,[8] however, should find a ready màrket in offices, homes, and restaurants that now have satisfactory heating[10] equipment.

We shall await with interest the report of our men when they return from Springfield. You may feel[12] certain that any opportunity for steady business during our dull season will receive serious[14] consideration.

Yours truly,   (150)

164

Randall and Peck, Inc.
35 Draper Avenue
Rochester 10, New York
Gentlemen:

Thank you for your letter of March 26. We are pleased to know that your firm will be represented[2] at our factory demonstration on April 8 and 9.

Reservations have been made for your men at the Arlington[4] Hotel on Broad Street. Everything possible will be done to make their visit to Springfield comfortable,[6] enjoyable, and profitable.

Our new Scott portable room-cooler is the result of years of experience[8] and hundreds of tests made with all types and styles of equipment. From your experience with us, you will know[10] that we do not rush a product to the public. It must be inspected, tested, and approved according to our[12] high standards.

Very truly yours,   (125)

165

The Scott Company
93 Carpenter Street
Springfield 7, Massachusetts
Gentlemen:

We are very much interested in the report of our men who attended your factory[2] demonstration. Mr. Blake believes that his sales force can bring in orders that will justify the addition of this[4] type of equipment to our line.

We are, therefore, enclosing our purchase order No. 1712 to confirm[6] the tentative order which Mr. Blake left with you.

Your recommendation that we make use of a factory[8] mechanic in our service department until our men are thoroughly familiar with this type of equipment[10] seems very sensible. If you can arrange to have a man from the factory here about May 15, we[12] shall be ready to profit from his visit.

Yours truly   (130)

166

William H. Webster & Company
92 Miller Street
Elmira, New York
Gentlemen:

Our 19.... catalogue was mailed to you yesterday. When you have examined it, we know you[2] will agree that we have provided a real service book for your office.

You will see at a glance that this is not[4] an ordinary catalogue. It is different because actual office problems are considered from your[6] point of view. You will find it profitable to compare your present office methods and equipment with the[8] progressive methods and equipment described in this new book. You will learn that our modern methods, equipment, and supplies[10] will be helpful to you in solving your office problems.

Our service department is always ready to work[12] with you on your own particular office needs.

Very truly yours,   (132)

167

William H. Webster & Company
92 Miller Street
Elmira, New York
Gentlemen:

Our 19.... office service book has been in your office for several weeks and we are confident[2] that it has given you many valuable ideas.

The necessity for economy has[4] brought about many changes in office methods, equipment, and layout in recent years. Offices that were modern[6] ten years ago may be entirely out of date today. We feel certain that your office efficiency can[8] be increased and your office costs reduced by a careful study of this complete service book.

You may buy from this[10] catalogue with the utmost confidence. Every item is clearly described and plainly priced. Our 45[12] years of experience and honest service to American business are your guarantee.

Very truly yours,   (130)

168

H. C. Taylor & Company
105 Beekman Street
New York 2, New York
Gentlemen:

Our office will be moved to a new building about June 1.

Since we desire to derive the greatest[2] possible benefit from our new office space, we are considering the use of counter equipment.

We believe[4] that we can save space and time by using a counter to separate our reception space from our working space[6] and by including our office files in this counter. The additional table space that a counter would provide[8] would be very useful in our business for the study of large building plans with our customers.

We have decided,[10] therefore, to take advantage of your free layout service. Please have your representative arrange to call[12] during the week beginning March 4.

Very truly yours,   (130)

169

William H. Webster & Company
92 Miller Street
Elmira, New York
Gentlemen:

Thank you for your letter of February 21 and for the opportunity to work with[2] you in preparing the layout of your new office.

Mr. James Quinn, a man with considerable experience[4] in planning offices, will be ready to help you on Monday, March 4. We are placing at Mr. Quinn's disposal[6] all our planning facilities. For over 35 years this department has been planning offices and solving office problems for almost every kind of business. From every part of the country, our[10] trained men, who are in daily contact with the problems of office operation, are sending in ideas for[12] improvement.

Your new office will profit by this unusual service.

Very truly yours,   (136)

170

H. C. Taylor & Company
105 Beekman Street
New York 2, New York
Gentlemen:

Mr. Quinn left with us last week a floor plan for our office and a list of specifications for the[2] counter equipment. We found his assistance very helpful and have studied his suggestions carefully.

Mr.[4] Quinn recommends your fireproof counter file units as the first choice and your regular counter units as the[6] second choice. Since we now have a large, fireproof safe in our office, this additional expense does not seem necessary.[8]

We are, therefore, enclosing our purchase order for the counter equipment with your regular units.[10]

The contractor says our new office space will be ready on May 15. You must, therefore, plan to install this new[12] equipment not later than May 22.

Very truly yours,   (131)

171

*

William H. Webster & Company
92 Miller Street
Elmira, New York
Gentlemen:

Thank you for the purchase order which you enclosed in your letter of March 14. We are pleased that we[2] have been given the responsibility of planning your new office.

As a result of our long experience,[4] we feel it is our duty to urge you to reconsider your decision not to install fireproof files. Can[6] you afford to be without day and night protection for your correspondence, contracts, and other valuable[8] business papers that are the lifeblood of your business? Although modern buildings are built as nearly fireproof[10] as possible, no building can be more fireproof than its contents.

Since all business records deserve complete protection,[12] please read the enclosed booklet, Assets or Ashes.

Very truly yours,   (133)

172

Mr. M. W. Lane
Lane Hardware Company
71 Sanford Street
Buffalo 2, New York
Dear Mr. Lane:

Thank you for your letter of February 8.

Our representative, Mr. Fred Perry, has[2] been instructed to call on you during the week beginning February 28. Mr. Perry will make[4] a definite appointment by telephone.

Our booklet listed only 60-cycle models because this is[6] the type most commonly ordered. However, we can supply 40-cycle motors in any model without[8] extra charge. Mr. Perry will discuss this matter with you in detail.

All reports indicate that when hot weather[10] comes there will be a strong demand for the new Bryant fans with their durable motors and attractive colors.[12] Demand should result in increased profits and we want you to have your share.

Very sincerely yours,   (137)

173

Mr. M. W. Lane
Lane Hardware Company
71 Sanford Street
Buffalo 2, New York
Dear Mr. Lane:

Yesterday we received Mr. Perry's report of his visit to your store on March 3. We are[2] grateful for your order because it proves that you were impressed by the style and quality of Bryant fans.

Mr.[4] Perry informed us that you believe you can develop considerable business where current is produced[6] by privately-owned power plants. Certainly this field has been neglected. There is a business opportunity[8] for you in every farm and camp in your vicinity having its own electric plant.

We suggest that[10] you permit us to work with you after you have made a survey in your locality to learn what type of current[12] is produced by these small power plants.

Very sincerely yours,   (131)

174

Bryant Manufacturing Company
173 Broadway
Albany 3, New York
Gentlemen:

The shipment of Bryant fans arrived yesterday in good condition.

We have given much thought to the[2] possible market for electric fans in camps and on farms in this vicinity which are not served by the local[4] power company. It does not seem wise to enter this field because our survey shows that there are only a[6] few privately-owned electric plants. There will be a real opportunity for additional business[8] when the power lines are extended to reach these farms and camps.

Now that we are getting ready for hot weather, will[10] you be good enough to send us some advertising material for use in our windows and on our counters?[12]

Very truly yours,   (123)

175

Mr. M. W. Lane
Lane Hardware Company
71 Sanford Street
Buffalo 2, New York
Dear Mr. Lane:

Advertising displays for your windows and counters, as well as a supply of folders showing[2] the strong selling points of Bryant electric fans, will reach you in a few days. Mr. Perry requested this material[4] for you in his report, but labor trouble in the printing plant caused some delay.

In addition to[6] this material, we can offer you cuts for newspaper advertising and copy for local radio[8] programs. Several of our customers have made profitable use of our radio advertising scripts.

Please [10] let us know what additional material you can use. We are eager to convince you that the quality[12] of our service is just as high as the quality of Bryant fans.

Very sincerely yours,   (136)

176

Mrs. Carl Miller
192 Arizona Street
Butte, Montana
Dear Madam:

We don't know of a more interesting store than this for the mothers of boys, and we want you to know it better[2] than you do.

While economy of cost is a prime consideration both with you and with us, we do not permit[4] ourselves to lose sight of the attractiveness of style and proper fit in making clothing for children.

We don't know[6] of any other cause that has so happily struck the exact balance between what a boy ought to wear and what[8] his clothing ought to cost.

It will be a great pleasure to show you what we have done for the little fellows if you[10] will give us that opportunity.

Very truly yours,   (106)

177

Mr. Joseph C. Brenton
Advertising Manager
The Rodman Company
Indianapolis, Indiana
My dear Mr. Brenton:

I have been intending to write you ever since I returned from the Boston Convention.

They say that the time to[2] advertise is when you want more business.

If you are interested in getting in closer touch with your buyers[4] or in decreasing your proportionate selling cost, I should like to show you what we have done for others.

I have[6] been wondering if a booklet telling about your proposition just the way you would tell it to me, if I were[8] a prospective buyer, would not be of value just at this time.

The facilities of this office backed by eight[10] years' experience in this territory are at the other end of either of your telephones, there in front[12] of you.

Yours truly,   (121)

178

Mr. Charles F. Newton
1415 Broadway
New York, N. Y.

My dear Mr. Newton:

Two heads working together often produce great results.

The knowledge you have gained from experience in your business[2] has an established value; the knowledge gained from my eighteen years' experience in planning, writing and executing[1] form letters would be valuable to you.

The two combined would be sure to produce greater results in your[6] mail campaigns.

Read the enclosed booklet, make an appointment, and then let us talk it over.

Yours very truly,   (76)

179

Mr. Jerome B. Johnson
Automotive Equipment Co.
1415 Bedford Avenue
Brooklyn, N. Y.

Dear Mr. Johnson:

Today we received a letter from a dealer saying he has sold 509 Fisk Inner Tubes in the[2] past seven months to car owners and up to the present time has not received a request for adjustment or the[4] suspicion of a complaint.

A dealer from another state writes:

"Fisk Tubes are longer lived than any others. We[6] have a great many users whose Fisk Tubes are over four years old and the rubber is still bright and lively."

Fisk Inner[8] Tubes are unequaled. TWENTY-FIVE THOUSAND perfect to ONE imperfect is the record. The reason— these[10] tubes are PURE para rubber with only enough sulphur to vulcanize. They do not stretch out of shape and cannot[12] deteriorate.

Yours very truly,   (124)

180

William A. Hodges & Son
32 Bryant Street
Allentown, Pa.
Gentlemen:
Thank you for your letter of March 21.

Our shipping department informed us this morning that your annual[2] seed order will be ready for shipment on Thursday March 25. You should, therefore, have your new stock within[4] a few days.

Yours very truly,   (40)

181

Mr. Clarence Gorman, Principal
Senior High School
Paterson, New Jersey
Dear Mr. Gorman:
It was a pleasure to learn from your letter of January 17 that our Mr. Brennan was so successful[2] in the presentation of the assembly program at your school.

Most people today, of course, realize the[4] need for teen-age driver training from the safety point of view. Too many, however, have failed to recognize the[6] cost in property damage and increased automobile insurance rates. Mr. Brennan's materials show clearly[8] that high school driver training classes have become a sound investment from every angle.

In several places[10] the school program has led to requests from parent-teacher and local service clubs. We shall be glad to arrange a[12] date upon request.

Yours very truly,   (125)

182

Bryant Manufacturing Company
173 Broadway
Albany 3, New York
Gentlemen:

We are making our plans for next summer and are interested in your booklet concerning the Bryant[2] electric fans.

Our problem of selecting electric fans is complicated by the fact that both[4] 60-cycle and 40-cycle currents are used in this city. This means that two complete stocks must be carried if[6] we are to be in a position to give satisfactory service to our customers. In your booklet we[8] note that all models require 60-cycle current. We should like to have information concerning this matter.[10]

We shall be glad to have your representative call during the week beginning February 28. A[12] definite appointment should be made by telephone.

Very truly yours,   (132)

183

Mr. C. H. White
The Emerson Company
215 Court Street
Lynn 8, Massachusetts
Dear Mr. White:

Is your bookkeeping staff still using a pen? Are they spending long hours on bookkeeping records while[2] other important matters receive little attention?

The increase in business activity requires speed,[4] accuracy, and simplicity in all bookkeeping work. Modern business demands modern bookkeeping equipment.[6] The Bragg Bookkeeping Machine, described in the enclosed booklet, was built to meet the needs of retail stores.

After[8] you have read this booklet, let us study your needs and show you how the Bragg machine will actually do the[10] bookkeeping work in you store.

Please give us this oportunity to help you by mailing the enclosed card now. Our [12] service is free.

Sincerely yours, (125)

184

Mr. C. H. White
The Emerson Company
215 Court Street
Lynn 8, Massachusetts

Dear Mr. White:

No two men are alike.

One man jumps to a conclusion without careful consideration of[2] all available information. Another man examines each fact, checks every claim, and profits from the[4] experience of others. Then he makes his decision.

Two weeks ago our booklet, LIVE RECORDS, went out to you[6]. After reading it, you have, of course, made your decision carefully.

We should like to aid you. You can check in your[8] store each point and every claim of the Bragg machine. Booklets and showroom demonstrations are interesting, but[10] actual performance on the job is convincing.

Mail the enclosed card today and we will place a Bragg Bookkeeping[12] Machine in your store.

Sincerely yours, (127)

185

The Bragg Equipment Company
275 Draper Avenue
Boston 11, Massachusetts

Gentlemen:

Your letter and the Booklet, LIVE RECORDS, reaches us at a time when our bookkeeping is a matter[2] of real concern. The booklet, therefore, has received our careful attention.

Our office force was reduced last year. The[4] marked development of business in the past year has increased the importance of our bookkeeping problem. For[6] a long time we have been considering the use of bookkeeping machines. We are not yet convinced, however, that[8] such a large outlay of money would result in a satisfactory return. Nevertheless, something must be[10] done to relieve the pressure in our work.

Will you kindly have your representative call on Monday, May 10, at[12] ten o'clock, to discuss arrangements?

Very truly yours, (130)

186

Mr. C. H. White
The Emerson Company
215 Court Street
Lynn 8, Massachusetts

Dear Mr. White:

Thank you for your letter of April 30.

Your interest in the Bragg Bookkeeping Machine indicates[2] that you realize the necessity for improving your bookkeeping system. A good system should handle[4] increasing volume and also reveal business information accurately and promptly.

Mr. James[6] Walsh of our staff will call at your office at ten o'clock on Monday, May 10. Mr. Walsh is an expert in[8] retail-store records and we feel confident that your contact with him will prove very helpful.

Please remember that a[10] national business organization with an active research and service bureau stands back of Mr. Walsh[12] and the Bragg Bookkeeping Machine. This bureau serves our business friends without charge.

Sincerely yours, (137)

187

The Bragg Equipment Company
275 Draper Avenue
Boston 11, Massachusetts

Gentlemen:

More than ten days have elapsed since Mr. Walsh completed his study of our bookkeeping requirements.[2] His analysis was thorough and his report is being studied carefully.

Mr. Walsh left a machine for[4] a trial of two weeks. This is a short period in which to make a decision that will change habits developed[6] through the years. Moreover, an outlay of about $3,000 demands complete investigation.

Will[8] you leave this machine with us for one month? We are very anxious to know what changes in our office force would result[10] from the use of the machine, because we hesitate to make a radical change in our present staff.

Very[12] truly yours,   (122)

188

Mr. C. H. White
The Emerson Company
215 Court Street
Lynn 8, Massachusetts
Dear Mr. White:

We are glad to learn from your letter of May 28 that our survey of your bookkeeping needs[2] has impressed you. We were confident that Mr. Walsh would help you.

We shall be pleased to have you keep the Bragg Bookkeeping[4] Machine for one month as you requested.

Your consideration for your present employees is commendable.[6] Your purchase of the Bragg equipment will affect them favorably, since this new equipment will enable[8] your present force to handle your increasing business. All operating instructions will be given free by[10] our company. You will note that Mr. Walsh covers this point on Page 8 of his report.

Please call on us for[12] assistance at any time.

Sincerely yours,   (127)

189

Lane Hardware Company
71 Sanford Street
Buffalo 2, New York
Gentlemen:

Mark Twain once said, "Everybody talks about the weather and nobody does anything about[2] it." We want to help you do something about the weather in your town.

We are thinking of next summer and your[4] electric-fan business. As you know from experience, however, profits from summer business always depend[6] upon careful planning and buying during the winter months.

The enclosed booklet, DOING SOMETHING ABOUT THE[8] WEATHER, contains illustrations and specifications of our new models of fans for home and office. Page 10[10] shows the colors that may be used with home furnishings.

Bryant fans will increase your profits. Use the enclosed card to[12] tell us when our representative may call to help you.

Very truly yours,   (133)

190

Madison Lumber Company
107 South Street
Rutland, Vermont
Gentlemen:

The desire to keep up to date is today more than ever an important factor in American[2] life. People are spending money and will continue to spend money. If you do not want other concerns to[4] get your business and your profits, you must sell the public a new idea.

Many families never think[6] of driving old cars even though they are in excellent condition. Many families will not consider living[8] in old and unattractive houses. Old houses can be made into modern homes as the result of the Baker[10] sales promotion program. This service is absolutely free.

If you will mail the enclosed card, full information[12] will be gladly furnished without obligation on your part.

Very truly yours,   (135)

191

Madison Lumber Company
107 South Street
Rutland, Vermont
Gentlemen:

About two weeks ago an interesting Baker program was

offered to a dealer and accepted[2] by him. He lives in a city of about 15,000 population, in the state of Maine. His business[4] is very much like yours.

This particular plan permits the dealer to act as our local agent. It enables[6] him to obtain a complete Baker stock on short notice. It gives him all the advantages of a direct[8] mail campaign without the usual advertising costs.

To this dealer the Baker program was a golden[10] opportunity to become connected with a national advertising plan. This same offer is open[12] to you. May we have the privilege of telling you more about it?

Very truly yours, (135)

192

Madison Lumber Company
107 South Street
Rutland, Vermont
Gentlemen:

Every retail lumber dealer should be interested in our wood products. Your attention is[2] therefore again called to the Baker program. By featuring Baker products, it will be possible to secure[4] a profit and quick turnover of stock. These sales also will assist in selling many other lumber items[6] that you carry in your yard.

There is a very definite program of sales promotion connected with the[8] marketing of Baker materials. We should like to discuss this program with you, because we are confident[10] that you will be pleased with its many advantages. Just tell us that you are interested and we shall be glad[12] to go over the entire matter with you.

Very truly yours, (131)

193

Madison Lumber Company
107 South Street
Rutland, Vermont
Gentlemen:

The public has just so much money to spend. Much of this

money has been going to the automobile[2] industry. However, an automobile salesman recently told us that his strongest competitor is[4] now the lumber dealer who sells materials for building or modernizing the home. Certainly this statement[6] should be encouraging to you.

The Baker sales plan has been developed to assist you in getting your share of[8] the business. It sells the public the idea of better and more modern homes. The use of the plan will bring[10] the advice and experience of our advertising and sales departments into your office.

Information[12] about our program is yours for the asking. Your request places you under no obligation.

Very truly yours,   (140)

194

Madison Lumber Company
107 South Street
Rutland, Vermont
Gentlemen:

During good times we manufacture the next depression. During the depression we build for prosperity.[2] Almost all the installment accounts that were due when the decline started have now been paid. Finance companies[4] report that their collections were made without serious losses. These companies now have more money than they[6] can use, because the new accounts have not been started on a large scale.

You can help put this surplus money into[8] circulation by adopting the Baker sales promotion program. We are sure you will appreciate this[10] opportunity and will give the plan your careful consideration.

May we send a representative to talk[12] with you? He will call at your convenience.

Very truly yours,   (131)

195

Madison Lumber Company
107 South Street
Rutland, Vermont
Gentlemen:

For several weeks we have been sending you letters about the Baker sales promotion program. This[2] program includes the national advertising of Baker products in magazines that reach over thirteen million[4] persons.

You, however, should be more interested in the direct-mail campaign that reaches the builders in[6] your district at intervals of three weeks. This feature continues as long as you co-operate with us in our[8] sales campaign. There is no charge for this service. The work is handled entirely by our home office.

These are only[10] two of the many advantages to be gained by adopting the Baker plan. A word from you will bring full[12] information to your desk.

Very truly yours,   (127)

196

Allen Clothing Company
132 Webster Street
Akron 6, Ohio
Gentlemen:

Your order of August 15 for topcoats is greatly appreciated. We wish we could make[2] immediate shipment. There has been so strong a demand for these attractive styles that our factory has been working[4] twenty-four hours a day in an effort to fill all orders promptly.

Your request for an early delivery[6] will be given every consideration and the coats should be on their way to you within ten days. We will[8] follow this shipment with a tracer, so that there may be no delay in transit.

When you see the beauty of these[10] new coats, we feel confident that you will overlook the inconvenience caused by our inability to[12] send them to you at once.

Very truly yours,   (127)

197

Allen Clothing Company
132 Webster Street
Akron 6, Ohio
Gentlemen:

Our credit manager has just informed me that you have not yet sent us a check for $615[2] for the shipment of topcoats made to you on August 25. Inasmuch as we offered you the[4] usual terms of 2/10, n/30, we fail to understand your delay in making payment.

Surely our[6] merchandise must have been satisfactory or we would have heard from you. In fairness to us we ask that you settle[8] this account immediately.

We are now completing our winter stock. The overcoat patterns and styles are[10] unusually beautiful.

The prompt payment of your present account will make it possible for us to fill your[12] next order without delay.

Yours very truly,   (128)

198

Perry Manufacturing Company
720 Edison Street
Buffalo 3, New York
Gentlemen:

We are enclosing a check for $300 to be credited to our account. We had expected[2] to pay the full amount when the bill became due and regret that we are unable to send you a larger[4] amount at this time.

You will recall that the shipment of topcoats did not reach us until two weeks after[6] the date on which you promised delivery. This caused a delay in the display of our stock, which resulted in[8] a slowing up of sales. Collections, too, are still poor in this territory. Accordingly, we shall be unable[10] to pay the balance on this account before the first of next month.

We hope you will grant us this extension.

Very[12] truly yours,   (122)

199

Allen Clothing Company
132 Webster Street
Akron 6, Ohio
Gentlemen:

We thank you for your check for $300, which has been credited to your account. It is not² customary for us to grant extensions on accounts, as the terms indicated on the invoice are a definite⁴ part of our sales policy. We will make an exception in your case, however, because we believe that⁶ our delay in shipping your order must have caused you some inconvenience and loss of sales.

We request that you⁸ cooperate with us by paying the balance of $315 on the first of next month. It would¹⁰ be exceedingly wise for you to close this account in order to protect your credit standing with the bank.

Yours very¹² truly,   (122)

200

Allen Clothing Company
132 Webster Street
Akron 6, Ohio
Gentlemen:

Although today is the 15th of the month, we find that you have not yet paid the balance of² $315 due us, in spite of the fact that you promised to send us your check on the first. We must now insist⁴ that you take immediate steps to close this account.

You should realize that the margin of profit is very⁶ small on low-priced clothing. It is only by the prompt collection of bills that we can continue to give our⁸ customers quality merchandise at surprisingly low prices.

Place your check in the enclosed business reply¹⁰ envelope and save both of us the embarrassment of collecting this account by other methods.

Yours very¹² truly,   (122)

201

Allen Clothing Company
132 Webster Street
Akron 6, Ohio
Gentlemen:

We received your check for $302.70 this morning and have credited[2] it to your account. We note, however, that you have deducted 2 per cent from the amount of this invoice, although[4] this account is more than three months past due. Our terms of 2 per cent discount for payment in ten days are offered to[6] encourage the prompt settlement of accounts. If we allowed a discount after the maturity of an invoice,[8] we should defeat the very purpose for which the discount was established.

We feel sure that you will cooperate[10] with us by sending your check to cover the balance of $12.30 deducted in error.[12]

Yours very truly,   (123)

202

Miss Ruth Green
208 North Avenue
Baltimore 14, Maryland
My dear Miss Green:

The Drake Hotel is a comfortable and well-managed house, situated on a beautiful[2] piece of land in the hills of Bell Harbor. From the heart of Baltimore it can be reached by train or automobile[4] in less than an hour. Although it is near the city, it is far enough removed for rest and quiet.

Majestic[6] old trees and attractive walks add to the beauty of the grounds about the building. The extensive lawns reach to the[8] shore of Chesapeake Bay. An excellent beach and private bathhouses are available to those who enjoy the[10] water. Fishing and boating are always in season.

We extend to you and your friends a cordial invitation[12] to visit us.

Sincerely yours,   (126)

203

Miss Grace M. Jones
244 Garden Street
Baltimore 16, Maryland
Dear Miss Jones:

   As a result of many years of experience in managing hotels, we have succeeded in[2] making the Drake a home of close friendships. We offer you a great many opportunities to meet people both[4] in and out of doors.

   A series of concerts and dances, at no extra cost to you, is included in our program[6] of social events. You will find the Drake a source of real pleasure in the entertainment of your friends. The[8] public rooms and trained staff are at your service.

   We suggest that you read the enclosed folder and examine carefully[10] our schedule of rates. A few minutes of your time now will be well spent and may mean many hours of future enjoyment.[12]

Cordially yours,   (124)

204

Miss Helen H. Smith
109 Charles Street
Baltimore 12, Maryland
My dear Miss Smith:

   One cannot be a guest at the Drake without feeling the friendly spirit of the place. For that reason,[2] it is always a pleasure to come back to this comfortable, modern hotel.

   This is the impression of[4] those who have been guests at our hotel again and again. Their enthusiasm has prompted us to bring to your attention[6] our plans for the coming season.

   We have decided to keep the Drake open all year. Our reasonable[8] prices have placed within the reach of everybody the conveniences of a well-managed hotel.

   You[10] will find it well worth your while to see the Drake before you make definite plans for your next vacation.

Sincerely yours,   (120)

205

Mr. Frank A. Brown
633 Park Road
Baltimore 10, Maryland
My dear Mr. Brown:

Do you like golf? If so, you will enjoy a holiday visit to the Drake Hotel. Our golf[2] course is considered ideally planned for both the beginner and the experienced player. There is a thrill[4] to a game played on a course overlooking the water. The exercise in the open always means a better[6] appetite .

The Drake Hotel does a thorough job. The hungry golfer must be fed. The large dining room offers the[8] best of Southern cooking three times a day. The delightful grill provides for those who like to eat between meals.

A vacation[10] spent at the Drake means health and strength and a lighter spirit on your return to business.

Very sincerely[12] yours,   (121)

206

Miss Anna Roberts
778 Young Avenue
Baltimore 20, Maryland
My dear Miss Roberts:

The Drake Hotel offers so many opportunities for enjoyment that we wonder why[2] you have not visited us. Are you a lover of tennis or riding or hiking? The Drake makes provision for[4] all of these sports.

Five good tennis courts are open to our guests at no extra charge. You may rent or buy at our own[6] sport shop any equipment you may need.

Riding facilities are within easy reach of the Drake, and the Bell[8] Harbor Hills furnish lovely trails for both riding and hiking. One of the most popular trips at the Drake is the[10] climb to the top of the hill at the break of day.

A reservation card is enclosed.

Sincerely yours,   (117)

207

Mr. Henry S. James
59 Union Street
Baltimore 16, Maryland

My dear Mr. James

Will you not take a few minutes to examine the enclosed card showing the rates at the Drake[2] Hotel? Do you know of any other place where a visitor can get so much enjoyment at so little cost?[4]

Do not make the mistake of believing that the Drake is solely a vacation hotel. It is open throughout[6] the year. Some of our best friends are guests who drop in for tea or bridge or a concert. Our nearness to Baltimore makes[8] the hotel especially attractive to those who want to combine a pleasant drive with an evening of[10] entertainment.

One visit will convince you that the Drake should be on your recreation list.

Sincerely yours,   (118)

208

Mr. James A. Leonard
17 Chestnut Street
Boston 5, Massachusetts

Dear Mr. Leonard:

You will be graduated in June and will then have to make a decision as to how the[2] following months and years will be spent. Your choice of a business course in high school indicated that you wished to[4] prepare for a business position. There is no doubt that you have had excellent training during your course in[6] the high school business department. There are, however, many advantages to be gained from continuing[8] your study of business subjects through a short intensive course in the Foster School of Business.

Our representative[10] will be glad to talk with you without any obligation on your part. Just mail the enclosed card. No[12] postage is required.

Very cordially yours,   (128)

209

Mr. James A. Leonard
17 Chestnut Street
Boston 5, Massachusetts

Dear Mr. Leonard:

For fifty years the Foster School of Business has been training young men and young women for[2] success in business. Our thorough instruction and high standards have helped them to obtain good positions and rapid[4] promotion. Many leaders in commerce and industry received their business education in our classes.[6]

If a business career is your choice of a life work, the Foster School of Business can give you a start.[8] Our courses are planned for those who need immediate employment and also for those who wish to prepare themselves[10] for expert accounting or shorthand reporting.

You are invited to visit our school and talk with us about[12] your plans.

Very cordially yours, (126)

210

Mr. James A. Leonard
17 Chestnut Street
Boston 5, Massachusetts

Dear Mr. Leonard:

A letter which reached our desk this morning asks if we guarantee positions to our graduates.[2] Have you a similar question?

We do not guarantee positions. No school can stand behind such a guarantee.[4] We do, however, have good facilities for assisting our graduates to obtain employment.[c] Our years[6] of satisfactory service to business firms have convinced employers that our school provides excellent[8] preparation for office workers. Business men have learned that Foster graduates can do their work efficiently. Last[10] year we were able to place 82 per cent of our graduates.

We should be glad to talk with you about your[12] future plans. Why not pay us a visit?

Very cordially yours, (132)

211

Mr. James A. Leonard
17 Chestnut Street
Boston 5, Massachusetts
Dear Mr. Leonard:

Do you know that an intensive business course costs very little? The tuition rate in the² Foster School of Business is only $35 a month. Our courses vary in length from three months to⁴ two years. We offer a short course for the high school business graduate who seeks early employment. We also⁶ offer longer and more complete courses which prepare for reporting and accounting positions.

A recent addition⁸ to our program is a two-year course in general business. This course is planned for those students who wish¹⁰ to continue their work in business management.

A catalogue will be sent to you on request. This booklet¹² contains full information about our school.

Very cordially yours,   (132)

212

Mr. James A. Leonard
17 Chestnut Street
Boston 5, Massachusetts
Dear Mr. Leonard:

Investigation shows that the earning power of the average high-school graduate is² actually increased if he has had the benefit of business training. You have acted wisely in preparing⁴ yourself for a business position. Your high-school course has provided you with excellent instruction⁶ and the use of modern equipment.

There are some things to be gained, however, by further study in the Foster⁸ School of Business. A short intensive preparation for immediate employment, or a longer course preparing¹⁰ for more responsible positions may be had in our school.

The service of our placement bureau is offered¹² free of charge. Our business reputation will be of great assistance to you in obtaining employment.¹⁴

Very cordially yours,   (145)

213

Mr. James A. Leonard
17 Chestnut Street
Boston 5, Massachusetts
Dear Mr. Leonard:

Since we have not heard from you, we assume that you have already obtained satisfactory[2] employment. A position at this time gives you an income, but will it assure you of rapid advancement without[4] further study? If not, let us suggest regular attendance at our night classes. The cost of night school is[8] only $15 a month and you can earn while you study.

Many of our night courses are taught by business[8] men who are associated with leading firms here in Boston. It would be well worth your while to study under[10] the direction of these experienced business men. Their instruction is based on actual business[12] practice.

An application blank is enclosed for your convenience.

Very cordially yours,   (130)

214

Graham Distributing Company
125 Hudson Street
Newark 12, New Jersey
Gentlemen:

Thank you for the order that Mr. Brown has just sent in. We are glad that you consider it worth while[2] to wrap 20,000 blankets in Transpar. This same good business judgement should tell you to give serious thought[4] to the use of Transpar for the remainder of your fall and winter stock.

Your attention is again called to the[6] use of small Transpar envelopes for the protection of samples. These inexpensive envelopes are available[8] in several sizes, and we know you will find them a valuable addition to your selling department.[10]

We want Transpar to serve you in every department of your business. Why not use it to protect your[12] men's sport shirts?

Yours very truly,   (125)

Graham Distributing Company
125 Hudson Street
Newark 12, New Jersey

Gentlemen:

We are writing to our envelope manufacturers for prices on envelopes suitable for[2] your samples. Just as soon as we hear from them, we will write to you again.

Your experience with the blankets will,[4] we feel certain, further prove to you the great value of Transpar as a clean, protective wrapper that helps to increase[6] sales.

In our general office we have a display room containing a most complete display of products wrapped[8] in Transpar. One of your blankets would be a very welcome addition to this display. If you care to send us[10] one, together with your invoice, which we will pay promptly, we shall be very glad to have you do so.

Very truly[12] yours,   (121)

Graham Distributing Company
125 Hudson Street
Newark 12, New Jersey

Gentlemen:

If you were to question the clerks in your stores, they would tell you that a customer always says, "Be sure[2] to give me a clean one."

Mr. Brown has already made certain special suggestions for your mail-order business[4] and he has written to the Johnson Manufacturing Company about the blankets. However, omitting[6] for the moment this particular problem, why not start now with Transpar in your retail stores? Other leading stores[8] are enthusiastic in their support of it.

Any articles that you care to send us will be wrapped promptly[10] and returned with suggestions and prices. Perhaps these new packages will help to bring your fall and winter lines more[12] in tune with modern practice.

Very truly yours,   (128)

217

Graham Distributing Company
125 Hudson Street
Newark 12, New Jersey

Gentlemen:

We have just read one of the letters telling of your special offering of sport shirts. Why not wrap these[2] shirts in Transpar? Your customers associate this clean, protective wrapper with a product of superior[4] value.

Thirty-two million advertisements are telling the story of Transpar. Thousands of your customers have[6] read these advertisements. Many of them now prefer to buy shirts wrapped in Transpar. The more Transpar you use, the greater[8] your benefit from this national advertising campaign.

If you will tell us whether you will need Transpar[10] for long-fold or short-fold shirts, prices will gladly be furnished.

By the way, have you considered putting samples in[12] envelopes like the one attached?

Yours very truly, (129)

218

Graham Distributing Company
125 Hudson Street
Newark 12, New Jersey

Gentlemen:

Have you ever considered the many advantages resulting from wrapping your various products[2] in Transpar? Shouldn't you like to talk with one of our men about it? He would discuss the whole matter with you and[4] would suggest ways and means of wrapping your goods attractively.

In your mail-order business, Transpar will meet an[6] actual need. It is no longer a luxury but a real necessity for the proper display of many[8] types of clothing. In fact, it may be used for every article of merchandise in your stores. Quantity[10] buying makes the cost of little importance.

We would suggest that you write us and set a definite time for our[12] salesman to call on you.

Yours truly, (126)

219

Graham Distributing Company
125 Hudson Street
Newark 12, New Jersey
Gentlemen:

Mr Brown, who represents us in your territory, has been asked to visit you at his early[2] convenience. In the meantime, if we can be of further help, please feel entirely free to write us.

Textiles and[4] clothing of all kinds are being wrapped in Transpar. Leaders in modern dry-goods merchandising are strong in their praise[6] of it. They have an eye to profit as well as to the better appearance of the merchandise on their display[8] counters. You may rest assured that your feeling will be the same as theirs, and the use of Transpar will give you the[10] reputation of selling quality goods.

"Transpar" on a shirt is the same as "Sterling" on silver.

Yours truly,   (119)

220

Mr. R. B. Sampson
14 West Street
West Union, Iowa
Dear Sir:

If your watch goes out of commission while you are away this summer, just pack it in a cigar box filled with newspaper,[2] and express to us, and it will receive our prompt attention. This method of transportation is perfectly[4] safe, and it is much better to have your watch handled by experts.

If you desire it, we will send a watch for[6] you to use by return express.

We do only the very best work, and our prices are very reasonable.[8]

We want to take care of your watch, and we will guarantee satisfactory results.

Respectfully yours,   (95)

221

Martin Manufacturing Company
15 South Wabash Avenue
Chicago, Illinois
Gentlemen:

Does your filing system ever go on a strike?

Does it ever refuse to give up instantly the information[2] that you know it holds?

Unless your filing devices minimize the moves necessary in transacting and[4] recording business, they make you a victim and not a master of details.

Your valuable papers and records[6] must not only be safe, but must be instantly available in order to facilitate and accelerate[8] the despatch of business.

Our cabinets are built for usefulness and you can select and arrange a cabinet[10] to suit your exact requirements, and not have to adjust your requirements to suit the cabinet.

The enclosed[12] card filled out and mailed to us will bring information helpful to you.

Yours very truly,   (132)

222

Mr. James Hepburn
141 Henry Street
Brooklyn, N. Y.
Dear Sir:

On looking over our records this week, we find that you have failed to renew your susbcription to Radio Guide[2] and we assure you we regret this very much. Our two previous letters to you expressed our appreciation[4] of having you as a subscriber and pointed out the many entertaining, enlightening and beneficial[6] features and departments in Radio Guide and explained to you our anxiety in having you remain[8] with us as a regular subscriber. In the absence of any word from you to date, we still wish to know[10] of your interest in Radio Guide. If you have decided to cancel your subscription, we would like to know[12] whether or not you intend purchasing it each week at a newsstand. Likewise, we are concerned as to just why you[14] have decided to discontinue your subscription, and will appreciate it greatly if you will be so good[16] as to write and tell us about it. Your suggestions will help us to issue an improved publication in the[18] future. However, we do hope you will reconsider and forward your renewal so that we may again enter[20] your name on our list as one of our friends and subscribers. Permit us to thank you in advance for your favorable[22] action.

Sincerely yours,   (223)

223

Mrs. Robert Ford
316 Center Street
East Orange, New Jersey
Dear Mrs. Ford:

We are pleased to learn that you recently purchased a R E X freezer. We can assure you that[2] proper use of this appliance will enable you to enjoy a better way of life.

Your R E X is more[4] than a convenience and a work saver. It is an investment, like your savings account in the bank. You will[6] find that it will pay dividends many times over its initial cost.

The inclosed booklet will introduce you[8] to your new electric servant. First we urge you to read carefully the instructions that came with your freezer. Then[10] we advise you to make a thorough study of the booklet and to follow with confidence the suggestions which[12] it contains.

Yours truly,   (123)

224

Mr. John R. Hudson
428 Morris Street
Troy 14, New York
Dear Mr. Hudson:
We are very glad to welcome you as the new representative
for R E X freezers in² Troy. We know you will enjoy working for a company which has the experience and the skill to
produce⁴ equipment that gives so much satisfaction.

Our customers will look to you for help in the choice and
care of their⁶ freezers. The territory to which you have been
assigned is one where our products are in great demand.
You should⁸ therefore find your duties as an agent of our
firm both interesting and profitable.

Any product¹⁰ is only as good as the factory and organization behind it. You may at all times rely on¹² the cooperation
of our home office.

                              Sincerely yours,   (131)

225

Miss Ruth Hall
842 Madison Avenue
Washington 7, D. C.
Dear Miss Hall:
Recently we wrote thanking you for the recipe you sent
us. We promised to let you know² what we would do with
the material as soon as we had made our final decision.

So many readers have⁴ expressed a desire to exchange
recipes that we are making them available through neigh-
borhood food markets. Five selections which may⁶ be used

as a complete dinner menu will be sent to the stores each month. Watch for the special window[8] and counter displays.

We have, in addition, arranged to have a publisher print the collection in book form. You will,[10] of course, receive a copy of the first edition.

Thank you for your help in developing our program.

                                     Cordially yours,[12]

                                                          (120)

226

Central Food Market
165 North Street
Rutland, Vermont
Gentlemen:

Your store is one of those chosen to receive a free advertising service from CAREER WOMEN on the first[2] of each month.

This service is designed to feature those products which are used in the favorite recipes sent to[4] us by our subscribers. Each month you will receive a counter display and material for both a window arrangement and[6] a newspaper advertisement.

We shall also send you a supply of leaflets containing the five recipes selected for the month.[8] You may want to inclose these leaflets with your monthly statements or include them in your deliveries, as other grocers[10] are doing.

We hope that this program will appeal to your customers and increase your food sales.

                                     Very truly yours,[12]

                                                          (120)

227

Mr. John B. Williams
24 South Oxford Street
Brooklyn, New York
My dear Mr. Williams:

No two men are alike.

You have individual requirements in dress. You desire cloth-ing that will add to your[2] appearance, not detract from it. Here is where tailoring skill comes to your assistance.

The designing in our shops[4] is under the personal direction of a member of the firm who devotes all his time and energy to[6] this work. He has an enviable reputation for producing clothing of rare distinction.

Making—not selling[8]—clothing is our business. A garment that is made right sells itself. If we make you one suit you are sure to come[10] to us when you want another.

If you desire to have the best there is, come in and see us.

Yours very truly,   (116)

228

Mr. Charles Robinson
56 Pacific Avenue
San Francisco, California
Dear Sir:

I often think most of us fail to appreciate the blessings of the age in which we live. The world has moved ahead[2] so fast in the last few years that the wildest dreams of the most imaginative writers of fiction not only[4] have been equalled, but in many cases far surpassed. When I was a boy my father's home and those of our neighbors[6] were heated with wood in great iron stoves. Now our homes are heated from a central plant with steam which comes on and[8] goes off at any desired temperature at the will of a delicate thermostat. At night our rooms were lit[10] up with kerosene lamps; now we press a button or turn a switch and our rooms are flooded with light generated[12] from the harnessed energy of a flowing river and reaching us across the miles by means of wires buried beneath[14] the ground or strung on poles high in the air. To go to the neighboring town and back was a day's journey, whereas[16] now it takes but a few minutes, thanks to the automobiles that move swiftly forward at our command. News of the[18] world came to us once a week in a paper printed in a distant city. Now we hear the important events[20] of the day every few minutes through the medium of the marvelous radio. Journeys that took months are[22] now accomplished in a few hours by means of great airplanes that fly beyond the reach of storm and cloud. Truly, how wonderful[24] it is to be alive in such an age—an age that gives advantages to the humblest individual[26] far beyond the imagination of a Homer or a Shakespeare.

Sincerely yours,   (273)

229

Mrs. James Parker
572 Hill Avenue
Perry, New York
Dear Mrs. Parker:

As a special favor to CAREER WOMEN, would you send us a copy of your favorite cooking[2] recipe? This may seem to be an unusual request. We make it because cooking methods have changed.

We are living[4] in the age of the electric kitchen, frozen foods, and prepared mixes. People still like to eat, however, and women[6] like to cook. We believe that some of the best cooks are business women who manage their homes as efficiently,[8] no doubt, as they do their offices. They have learned to plan meals that are timesaving as well as wholesome.[10]

If you have a dish of which you are particularly proud, won't you tell us about it?

Cordially yours,[12]   (120)

230

Mrs. Ruth Adams
27 Spring Street
New York 10, New York
Dear Mrs. Adams:
We have your letter of June 10 informing us that your
R E X freezer does not[2] operate as well as it formerly did.
We are sorry to receive this news and sincerely regret that[4]
our equipment is causing you any trouble.

Your letter has been referred to Mr. James Trent, our service[6] manager, who is giving it his personal attention. In
fact, Mr. Trent has already arranged to have one[8] of his
expert technicians call at your home next Friday morning
to inspect your freezer and to make[10] any necessary adjustments.

There will be no charge for this service, which is covered
by our one-year guarantee, unless[12] some damaged parts
have to be replaced.

Very truly yours,   (129)

231

Mr. R. S. Woods
People's Department Store
Aurora, Illinois
Dear Mr. Woods:
Do you have a mailing list?
Good!
Let us know how many names you have so that we can
cooperate with you in[2] selling the York Silks to every woman
in your viciny who is likely to buy silks.
How?
Simply by[4] having you tell her the same story we have been
telling you. We make this easy for you by giving you as many[6]

booklets, like the enclosed, as you need to go round your list. That will mean a lot of additional business for[8] you. Not only that, but it will make your store known as the silk store of your community—a reputation worth[10] striving for.

But read the booklet. Yours will bear your imprint on the front and back covers, and by sending it by mail[12] you will reach your customer when she is at rest and her mind receptive. It will not go the way of other booklets[14] because it comes direct from you and she knows there is something important in it for her.

Then, too, it will reach[16] her after she has seen the merchandise envelopes and signs in your store and possibly the silk itself. In this[18] way York Silk is not a stranger but a familiar friend introduced by one in whom she has confidence. She learns[20] all its good points and you fortify her with facts and evidence about the superiority of York Silk[22] and the weak points of others so that when she is ready to buy silk, she will want York and no other. All this information[24] she will remember and will be ready to impart to anyone who even mentions silk.

Think[26] what this will mean to your store.

The merchandise envelopes, booklets, signs, electrotypes of advertisements, and other[28] selling helps will be forwarded as soon as possible after you take the agency.

Write for it before the[30] advance in prices which takes effect December 15, and we will confine it to you for your town.

Yours truly,　　　　　　　(318)

232

Messrs. Brown & Schenck
126 East 19th Street
Bangor, Maine

Gentlemen:

For some reason you have not recently favored us with much of your business. We wonder why. You know how you feel[2] about a case of this kind. You have a line of goods, well assorted, prices right, courteous salesman, and for no[4] apparent reason you have received no orders from a desirable customer. Don't you begin to wonder[6] what is wrong?

Well, that is just the way we feel about it; every reason why you should buy from us, still no business[8]. Won't you help us out and tell us why?

You can do a nice business with us if we get together. We can help[10] you a great deal if you will write us, explaining why.

Yours truly, (109)

233

Mr. George Williams
91 State Street
Albany 1, New York
Dear Mr. Williams:
Mr. John R. Hudson has just been appointed as the representative for R E X freezers in[2] your territory. He is planning to visit your store the first week in August in order to assist[4] you in selecting the freezers you would like to have in stock this year.

Our supply of merchandise is greater[6] now than it has been for many months. We urge you, therefore, to take advantage of this situation and be[8] prepared to meet the current demand.

We are very fortunate that Mr. Hudson has agreed to join our staff. You[10] will find that he is an outstanding man in his field who will be able to offer you many valuable[12] suggestions.

Very truly yours, (122)

234

Mr. John Bates
42 Washington Avenue
Garden City, New York
Dear Mr. Bates:

The National Oil Company has just opened a modern service station at the corner of[2] Third Avenue and Center Street. The very latest equipment for the efficient servicing of cars has been[4] installed.

You will be glad to know that at this convenient location you can obtain gasoline, oil, and standard[6] auto supplies of the highest quality at low prices. Competent and courteous attendants are prepared[8] to serve you 24 hours a day.

If you will present the enclosed card to our manager, Mr. Frank Jones, a[10] deduction of $2 will be allowed on any purchase made before the end of June.

Very truly yours,[12] (120)

235

Mr. John Martin, Manager
National Service Station
196 Madison Avenue
Rochester 13, New York
Dear Sir:

Within the next few months you may expect to receive requests for information concerning the new[2] tubeless tires that have recently been developed. There will no doubt be a great demand for these tires because their many[4] unusual features afford maximum riding comfort and ease of driving.

We plan to include in our stock[6] a complete line of this superior product. There may be some delay, however, as manufacturers are[8] having difficulty meeting the current demand.

A small shipment that may be used for display purposes should[10] reach you this week. Please inform your customers that we shall do our best to fill their orders promptly.

Cordially yours,[12]   (120)

236

Miss Ruth Long
188 Spring Street
Brooklyn 14, New York
Dear Miss Long:

Every automobile owner knows how necessary it is to equip his car with seat covers[2] in order to beautify and protect the interior.

If you are among those who demand the best in[4] fashion and wearing quality, we advise you to inspect the various styles available at National[6] Service Stations.

These covers are made of a plastic-coated material in red, blue, or green, and they are[8] expertly tailored. You will be delighted to know that their bright new look can be easily maintained with soap and water.[10]

We urge you to make your purchase within the next two weeks while our sale prices are still in effect.

Yours truly,[12]   (120)

237

Mr. Robert Carson, Manager
National Service Station
400 Broadway
Trenton 7, New Jersey
Dear Mr. Carson:

An old customer has written us complaining of the manner in which he was treated at[2] your service station.

This gentleman has purchased gasoline and oil from our company for at least ten years, and[4] he has always praised our service as well as the quality of our products. He now reports that one of your[6] attendants was extremely rude to him and even refused to clean the windshield of his car.

We must insist that you[8] impress upon your employees the importance of courtesy at all times. In these days of strong competition,[10] the dealer on the next corner will be only too glad to welcome the customer you lose.

Very truly yours,[12]   (120)

238

Mr. John Crosby
253 Madison Avenue
Elmira, New York
Dear Mr. Crosby:
At this time of the year many of our friends find that the activities of winter are[2] beginning to lose their appeal. A change of scenery for at least a few days seems to be upper-most in their thoughts.[4] We suspect that you too may be having this urge.

The Cooper Travel Bureau offers a choice of several[6] delightful ocean cruises, which have been planned for your complete enjoyment. The most popular of these trips are described[8] in the enclosed booklet. You will find pleasure in reading about the exciting and colorful ports which you will[10] want to visit.

Won't you call at our office for a detailed account of the tour of your choice?

Very truly yours,[12]   (120)

239

Miss Mary Faye
Hotel Hamilton
76 North Street
Utica 3, New York
Dear Miss Faye:
Thank you for the check for $100 covering the first deposit
on your tour of South[2] America. Your prompt payment has
enabled us to reserve a very desirable stateroom for you.

We[4] suggest that you obtain your passport as soon as possible. All other details will be handled in our office.[6]

Several pamphlets which describe interesting purchases
that can be made in each country are being mailed to you[8]
today. You will also receive a letter concerning the type of
clothing needed and the amount of luggage[10] allowed.

We assure you that this trip will prove to be an experience
you will never forget.

Cordially yours,[12]   (120)

240

Miss Ruth Carpenter
52 University Place
Syracuse 4, New York
Dear Miss Carpenter:
In response to your recent inquiry, I am sending you literature on a tour of[2] the West Indies. You mentioned that your
vacation period will be short. You may therefore prefer to
travel by[4] airplane.

The service on this particular tour is excellent. At each
stopover you will be met by an[6] experienced guide. He will
assume full responsibility for your pleasure and comfort

from the moment he greets[8] you at the airport until he
waves farewell to you as you board the plane to leave.

May I suggest that you make[10] reservations promptly so as
to be sure of accommodations at a time convenient for you.

Sincerely yours,[12]   (120)

241

Mrs. Robert Fairbanks
49 Water Street
Rochester 7, New York

Dear Mrs. Fairbanks:

You will soon receive a folder which gives full details of the
Annual Travel Show presented[2] by the leading travel agencies in this city. This is always a gala affair that everyone[4]
in this area is eager to attend.

Representatives from many countries of the world will be
present[6] to describe their native lands. Motion pictures will
also be shown of some of the most breath-taking scenery
that[8] can be found.

We would enjoy having you attend this event as a guest of
our organization. Two tickets[10] that will admit you and one
of your friends are enclosed.

We know that you will enjoy this occasion.

Cordially yours,[12]   (120)

242

Mrs. Thomas A. Harrison
408 North Street
Peekskill, New York

Dear Mrs. Harrison:

You have not visited our bookshop for several months and
we are concerned. Is it possible that[2] your last purchase
failed to please you?

Our records show that you have not used your charge account since April[4] 17, when you selected the book, JOURNEY THROUGH INDIA. We have been receiving so many requests for this volume that[6] we are not able to meet the demand.

In July we plan to open a gift wrapping department where the[8] work will be under the supervision of a former teacher of art. This service will be offered at no extra[10] cost.

Won't you write a note on the inclosed card telling us how we may serve you better.

Cordially yours,[12]   (120)

243

The Coleman Public Library
32 First Street
Spring Lake, New Jersey
Gentlemen:
You have allowed your account to exceed by a substantial amount the limit agreed upon in our original contract.[2] When you wrote us in January you promised that a small sum would be paid each month on your account.[4] Several months have now passed and we have not heard from you. Will it be possible for you to send[6] us your check for at least $200 by July 15?

We realize that because you are building a[8] new library you face many difficult financial problems. Our best advice, however, is that you reduce your current obligations by[10] making small, regular payments.

Please let us know your plans in order that we may help you.

Yours very truly,[12]   (120)

244

Mr. Edward Mason, Manager
St. Paul Hotel
95 Broad Street
Yonkers 3, New York

Dear Sir:

As chairman of the committee in charge of arrangements for the convention of the bookstore salesmen of this[2] section, I wish to thank you for the excellent service we received at the St. Paul Hotel. Your entire staff[4] helped to make our visit to your city a pleasant experience.

Several of our members who were present have expressed[6] their desire to hold future meetings at your hotel. This plan will be recommended to the president of our organization.[8]

Our regular meetings are held on the first Monday of each month promptly at noon. We require the use of[10] a conference room for about one hour after our luncheon. Will you be able to accommodate us?

                                        Very truly yours,[12]   (120)

245

Mrs. Charles Parker
500 Lincoln Square
Hudson, New York

Dear Madam:

We are pleased to learn of your interest in our new set of reference books for children. These[2] ten volumes are attractive in appearance and appealing in content.

They have been selling at $65, but this[4] week they are being offered to our charge customers at only $49 for the complete set.

Your children[6] will find in these books answers to many of their school problems. They will enjoy the style of writing as[8] well as the information that has been brought together in compact form. They will also be delighted with the many[10] beautiful pictures.

Why not decide today to take advantage of our special offer before the time limit expires.

Yours truly,[12]　　　　　　(120)

246

Baker Brothers, Inc.
26 Market Street
Philadelphia 16, Pennsylvania
Gentlemen:
Because of the rising cost of raw materials, we are obliged to increase the prices of our leather products.[2] The higher prices will apply to all orders received on or after March 1.

This advance notice is being sent[4] to you so that you may take advantage of the opportunity to save money. We suggest that you place your[6] order while the current lower prices are still in effect.

A large volume of business will no doubt reach us[8] before the end of next month and there may be a delay in some of our deliveries. We therefore urge[10] you to determine your requirements within the next ten days and let us fill your needs at once.

Yours truly,[12]　　　　　　(120)

247

Mr. Henry Brooks
782 Madison Avenue
New York 5, New York
Dear Sir:

We have not received your check for the leather handbags purchased from us on October 10, 1955.[2] Perhaps you have overlooked the fact that payment was due within 30 days. If so, you will appreciate having[4] it called to your attention.

The items included in this order must have been satisfactory or you would have written[6] us. Is it possible that you have mailed your check but it has failed to reach our office?

We are[8] able to keep our prices low because we encourage our customers to pay promptly. Bad accounts are in this way[10] reduced to a minimum and the savings are passed along to you.

Won't you mail your remittance today?
Yours truly,[12]   (120)

248

Mr. William Jackson
Star Leather Goods, Inc.
34 Spring Street
Toledo 7, Ohio
Dear Mr. Jackson:

Please accept our thanks for the order you placed with us recently for 36 of our[2] genuine leather brief cases.

It is a pleasure to add your name to our list of customers. You may rest[4] assured that your order will receive our careful attention.

We are glad you supplied us with a statement of your[6] financial condition and the names of two references. Every effort will be made to complete as quickly as possible the[8] usual investigation on which credit terms are based.

We hope the slight delay in filling your order will not inconvenience[10] you. You will be notified as soon as we can give you a definite date for shipment.

Yours very truly,[12]   (120)

249

R. H. Dixon and Company
200 State Street
Rome, New York
Gentlemen:

Thank you for letting us know that you received the leather jewel cases ordered from us last month.

We[2] are sorry to learn that one of the cartons in this shipment was broken when it arrived and that six[4] of the jewel cases were damaged.

All items of merchandise leaving our factory are thoroughly inspected and carefully packed. We[6] have a receipt from our local freight agent showing that the ten cartons reached him in good condition. The damage[8] must therefore have occurred in transit.

You should take this matter up immediately with the railroad company and file a[10] claim. If a satisfactory adjustment is not made and we can be of service, please notify us.

Very truly yours,[12]   (120)

250

Mr. Charles Brown
46 School Street
Buffalo 12, New York

Dear Mr. Brown:

Welcome to Buffalo! We understand that you and your
family plan to live here. We know that[2] you will find our
city a pleasant and friendly place in which to work and live.

Our business demands that[4] we keep closely informed about
local conditions. If there is anything Lane Brothers can do
to help you in[6] getting settled, please come in and let us
know. We may be able to give you a helping hand in a[8]
number of ways.

You will,[8] no doubt, wish to establish credit in a local department store now that you are[10] a resident of this community. If so, we invite you to open an account with us.

Cordially yours,[12]   (120)

251

Mrs. John Brooks
23 College Road
Buffalo 5, New York

Dear Mrs. Brooks:

We wish to announce the opening of our Dry Cleaning Department. Our aim is to give service[2] of the best quality at
a moderate price. We shall appreciate your business.

Our truck will call for and deliver[4] garments either upon
request or according to a schedule arranged to suit you.
You may wish to select our economy[6] service. This provides
for a 20 per cent discount for work delivered to our store
and called for. The department[8] is open from 9 a.m. to
6 p.m. every day except Sunday.

136

We invite you to inspect the[10] building where our dry cleaning is done. It is located two blocks away, at 9 Market Street.

Cordially yours,[12]   (120)

252

Mrs. George Armstrong
29 State Street
Dunkirk, New York
Dear Mrs. Armstrong:
We are very sorry that the wrong merchandise was delivered to you in our shipment of January[2] 17.

The wall and woodwork cleaner that you ordered is being sent to you this morning. Our driver has been[4] instructed to pick up the plastic varnish that you received in error. Your account will be adjusted at once.

We[6] hope to have the opportunity soon to serve you in a more satisfactory manner. A representative will help choose exactly[8] what you want if you will telephone our Personal Shopping Service, Extension 25. We will try to exercise the[10] same good judgment and care that you would if you were here to make the selection yourself.

Sincerely yours,[12]   (120)

253

Central Bank and Trust Co.
72 Lexington Ave.
Yonkers 8, N. Y.
Gentlemen:
Mr. James R. King, who last year lived at 57 Lake Street, Yonkers, New York, has given your[2] name as a reference in opening an account with us.

It is our policy to investigate the financial rating of[4] our credit customers. We shall appreciate a statement from you regarding the general business reputation and responsibility of Mr. King.[6] We are ready to give him reasonable credit if your experience with him was satisfactory. Our regular form is enclosed[8] for your convenience.

The information that you supply us will be treated as strictly confidential. We shall be willing to[10] assist you in return with any of your investigations.

Thank you for this courtesy.

Very truly yours,[12] (120)

254

Atlas Storage Company
300 Madison Avenue
Albany 3, N. Y.

Gentlemen:

Mr. Charles Lee of White Plains, New York, has consulted with me in regard to the damages that he[2] sustained as the result of a recent automobile accident. A truck owned by you and operated by[4] your driver, John Adams, was involved. The collision occurred March 2, on Route 9, near the village of Hyde Park, New York.[6]

This accident, which resulted in the death of Mrs. Lee, was caused through the negligence of your driver. Mr. Lee,[8] therefore, expects to be compensated for his loss.

I suggest that you turn this letter over to your insurance[10] company so that the company may have a representative call at my office to discuss the matter.[12]

Yours truly, (122)

255

Mr. Joseph W. Lee
22 Grand Avenue
Yonkers 6, New York

Dear Mr. Lee:

Your father has filed a petition in the Surrogate's Court that he be appointed[2] administrator of your mother's estate. Your brother Harry and your sister Jane have signed waivers, consenting[4] to this appointment.

I assume it is agreeable to you that your father be appointed[6] administrator. I am, therefore, inclosing a waiver for you to sign so that it will not be necessary[8] to have special papers issued and served upon you.

Sign the form before a notary public and return[10] it to me in the inclosed stamped envelope. Please do this promptly so that we may proceed with various matters[12] in connection with the estate that must await your signature.

Yours truly,   (124)

256

Mr. Charles Lee
600 Central Avenue
White Plains, New York

Dear Mr. Lee:

I have obtained the bond that you, as administrator of the estate of your wife, must file with the[2] Surrogate's Court. Enclosed is the application, together with the original and two copies of the bond.[4]

Please fill in with care the information requested in question 5 of the application. You may estimate[6] the amount of cash that you have and your liabilities, if any.

Sign the application, together[8] with the original and the two copies of the bond, in the spaces marked X, in the presence of a[10] notary public.

The prompt return of all of the enclosed papers will enable me to proceed immediately[12] with the settlement of the estate.

Very truly yours,   (130)

257

Mr. Charles Lee
600 Central Avenue
White Plains, N. Y.
Dear Mr. Lee:

I am enclosing a form in order to have the War Savings Bond that was in your wife's name alone[2] reissued. After this paper has been signed by you in the presence of a qualified official, kindly[4] return it to me immediately.

You will note that I have provided that the bond is to be issued in your[6] name as administrator. It is not possible on this request to have the bond issued in any other form. If[8] you wish to name an additional individual on the new bond, you will have to file a separate request.[10]

This will conclude the transfer of all the bonds that were in your wife's name.

Very truly yours,   (116)

258

Mr. John Abbott
25 Broad Street
Lincoln, New York
Dear Mr. Abbott:

We are indeed glad to welcome your account to the First National Bank of Millington.

We value[2] your business and greatly appreciate the opportunity to be of service to you. It is our earnest[4] desire to be of help to you in more ways than by merely providing a safe place in which to deposit your[6] funds.

Our various departments, which offer the usual banking services, are here for your use. We shall be glad[6] to know that you are finding them of genuine benefit.

Please come in at any time you find yourself in a[10] situation that calls for a talk with one of our officers, no matter what the financial problem may be.

Cordially yours,[12]   (120)

259

Mr. Frank Clark, Pres.
First National Bank
260 Main Street
Millington 4, N. Y.
Dear Mr. Clark:

In your recent letter, you invited me to use the facilities of your bank. I stopped in last[2] Thursday and discussed the matter of a mortgage loan with your mortgage officer, Mr. Martin. He gave me the[4] necessary loan application forms.

I wish to enlarge my business and have taken a thirty-day option on a building[6] that will provide for the expansion desired. The third floor will be remodeled and made into two small apartments.

The[8] inclosed completed application gives the details of the proposed transaction. Will it be possible for you to consider this matter[10] at the next meeting of your Board of Directors so that I may take action promptly?

Yours truly,[12]   (120)

260

Mr. Thomas Adams
75 Market Street
Millington 5, New York
Dear Sir:
Kindly make an appraisal for the Veterans Administration
on behalf of John Abbott of Lincoln, New York. The[2] property is now a combination store and one-family dwelling at
the junction of Columbia Turnpike and Mill Road.

The[4] first floor of the building is to be used as a store for
automobile supplies, with a service and repair[6] department
in the rear. The second floor is to be remodeled for living
quarters for Mr. & Mrs. Abbott. Two[8] additional apartments
are to be made on the third floor for rental purposes.

Inclosed are the appraisal forms that have[10] been prepared
for your convenience. Please return them properly completed on or before next Monday.

Yours truly,[12]   (120)

261

Mr. John Abbott
25 Broad Street
Lincoln, New York
Dear Mr. Abbott:
Your application for a mortgage loan on the property located at Columbia Turnpike and Mill Road has[2] been approved in the amount of $10,000 based on our appraisal and
that of the Veterans Admin.

Monthly[4] payments of the amount specified will satisfy the
principal and interest requirements.

If you are able to complete the[6] transaction on this basis, bring or send in by registered mail your military discharge papers together with the appraisal fee[8] of $20.

You will be notified of the date on which the final papers are to be signed as[10] soon as our attorney has completed the title search and prepared the necessary papers.

Sincerely yours,[12]　　　　(120)

262

Brown Cabinet Company
92 Church Street
Newark 2, N. J.
Gentlemen:

Will you kindly send us information concerning the quick-freezing units that you are now offering for both city[2] and farm use? Many inquiries have been received because the food problem has aroused great interest in this method of[4] storing and preserving food supplies.

We have been a distributor of refrigerators in this area for years, and it is[6] only natural that we should want to be the leader in this field. You can see, therefore, why we should[8] like to make an agreement with a manufacturer of quick-freezing units to handle the distribution for the entire state.[10]

Complete information concerning models, prices and the details of your agency requirements will be appreciated.

Very truly yours,[12]　　　　(120)

263

Perry & Williams Company
15 Hamilton Ave.
Burlington, Vt.

Gentlemen:

As requested in your letter of January 4, you will soon receive complete information concerning the quick-freezing and[2] storage cabinets now in production. You will receive in addition some details of models still in the planning stage. You[4] realize, of course, that the market for quick-freezing equipment is just opening up and that changes and improvements will[6] come as the result of experience.

We expected to have our factory running up to schedule by this time, but[8] conditions beyond our control have limited production. The outlook for the months ahead, however, is promising.

We shall be able[10] to write you soon concerning the matter of an agency in Vermont.

Very truly yours,[12]   (120)

264

Perry & Williams Company
15 Hamilton Avenue
Burlington, Vt.

Gentlemen:

Since we wrote you last Saturday, the information you requested has been sent to you.

Our production problems have[2] been so puzzling that we have not been able to give much attention to our plan of distribution. Furthermore, we[4] have had very friendly business relations with a firm in Rutland for many years. It seems only just, therefore, that[6] this firm should be considered when our agency plan is established.

Please do not get the impression that we are[8] not interested in your request for the right to handle our products in Vermont. Your application is receiving our careful[10] attention, and we hope that arrangements can be made to have you distribute Brown products.

Very truly yours,[12]   (120)

265

Brown Cabinet Company
92 Church Street
Newark 2, N. J.

Gentlemen:

We were glad to receive the information concerning your quick-freezing and storage equipment that is now available. We[2] are also very much interested in the specifications for your new POLAR CABINET for farms. This unit should have strong[4] sales appeal in Vermont.

We are disappointed, however, because your price and delivery schedules are so indefinite. It is evident[6] that we can not make any plans without complete information.

It does not seem worth while, furthermore, for us to[8] consider Brown products seriously until we have assurance from you that a satisfactory agreement can be arranged.

Please give this[10] matter your prompt attention and let us know what you can offer.

Very truly yours,[12]   (120)

266

Bruce Book Store, Inc.
95 Dearborn Avenue
Pittsburgh, Pa.

Gentlemen:

An examination copy of Your Health and Your Food is in
the mail. Read it and we know you[2] will agree with us that
at last the relation of food to health appears in language
that can be understood[4] by everyone.

This book is full of useful information but technical terms
have been avoided. The author has no product[6] to sell except
health and happiness.

The book retails for $1.75. The price to you is $1.30.[8] In
addition to the usual discount of 25%, a special discount
of 10% will be allowed[10] on orders for 50 or more copies.

Now is the time to place this book in your window and on[12]
your counters.

Yours truly,   (124)

267

William A. Hodges & Son
32 Bryant Street
Allentown, Pa.

Gentlemen:

Thank you for your special order, which will be shipped at
once.

We have sent you 200 copies[2] of our new booklet, VICTORY
GROWS IN YOUR GARDEN, which has just come from
our printer.

This booklet will help[4] your customers to plan their Victory Gardens. Complete directions are given for preparing and preserving the food grown. Garden products[6] will relieve the strain on the food supply next summer. Preserved vegetables will be a welcome addition next winter to[8] the regular ration allowance of canned goods.

Everyone who has space for a garden has a definite duty this year[10] because Victory Gardens will help our national food program.

Additional copies of our booklet will be sent upon request.[12]
                                    Yours very truly,   (122)

                                    268

William A. Hodges & Son
32 Bryant Street
Allentown, Pa.
Gentlemen:
Recent news reports show very clearly that our nation faces a grim situation in the matter of food production.[2] We need more food than ever before in our history. We need it for our fighting men. We need it[4] for our allies. We need it to keep the folks at home healthy and strong. The food shortage is not[6] coming. It is here.

We hope our booklet, VICTORY GROWS IN YOUR GARDEN, will help to arouse people. We believe[8] Section 4, which starts on page 18, is very important. It shows the mistakes that were made last year and[10] tells how to avoid them this year.

Call on us for help at any time.
                                    Yours very truly,   (118)

269

Allison Publishing Company
25 Walnut Street
Philadelphia, Pa.

Gentlemen:

Please send us 60 copies of Your Health and Your Food by
Dr. Henry Ward.

We were very favorably[2] impressed by the reviews and even
more impressed by the book itself. We feel that we should
place it on[4] our shelves since it is a book that should be of
service to all Americans at this time.

The window[6] displays described in your booklet should increase sales. We can use display No. 3 in our large front
window and[8] display No. 7 in our small side window. Please
ship these displays with our order.

We have always found[10] that counter displays are effective
and we wonder if you have given this matter any consideration.

Very truly yours,   (119)

270

Bruce Book Store, Inc.
95 Dearborn Avenue
Pittsburgh, Pa.

Gentlemen:

Thank you for your letter of October 15. The books and window displays were shipped on Friday.

We appreciate[2] your order and your high opinion of our new
book, Your Health and Your Food. Although Dr. Ward is
an[4] authority in the field of nutrition, he has produced a

book so simply written that it is easily understood by[6] people with no scientific training. Words of praise are coming in from all sections of the country.

Several dealers agree[8] with your suggestion concerning counter displays. We shall, therefore, do our best to have some attractive material ready as soon[10] as possible. Please do not hesitate to tell us if there is anything else we can do to help you.[12]

Yours truly,   (122)

271

Bruce Book Store, Inc.
95 Dearborn Avenue
Pittsburgh, Pa.
Gentlemen:
The inclosed booklet tells the story of a very important book that is now being printed.

The author of[2] this book, Your Health and Your Food, has made a real contribution to the defense program, which demands health, energy,[4] and morale. He shows that millions of our people are badly nourished although we have the finest food supply of[6] any nation. He attacks this problem directly and develops in his readers an appreciation of the need for the best[8] possible nutrition for the money that they have to spend.

This book will be published early in October and, of[10] course, a copy will be sent to you. Selling this book will indeed be a public service.

Yours truly,   (119)

272

FINANCING A WAY OF LIFE

The Finance Business is an integral part of America's economic system. It provides working[2] capital for business . . . helps underwrite American ingenuity . . . makes available the essential funds[4] for development of new ideas . . . the manufacture of merchandise . . . it enables distributors and[6] dealers to buy and carry complete stocks of diversified lines . . . and, finally, makes it possible for the ultimate[8] consumer to purchase, on deferred payment terms, automobiles, household appliances, machinery,[10] etc., from dealers, distributors and manufacturers. The seller receives immediate cash, the[12] customer receives the merchandise without delay and pays monthly out of income.

America's vast industrial[14] growth and high standard of living can be attributed, in large measure, to mass production and distribution,[16] made possible by use of the time payment plan of buying and selling.   **(172)**

273

PUT AND CALL OPTION CONTRACT

European investors, large and small, have been using Stock Options in security markets for 100[2] years and longer ever since such markets were first organized. In this country, however, the rank and file investor[4] until recently has avoided the use of Put and Call Contract Options which he regards as a specialized[6] and complicated technique.

Actually, there is nothing either mysterious or difficult to[8] understand about a Stock Option. Essentially, it is a Contract, paid for in advance, in which the[10] holder has the right to buy, in the case of a Call Contract, or sell, in the case of a Put Contract, a specified[12] number of shares at any time within the period covered by the contract.

Consider the speculative[14] possibility first. Let us assume you feel that Horne and Company is low priced at $70 a share[16] and that it could advance to $85 a share in three months. To buy 100 shares under 70 per cent[18] margin rules would require a cash investment of $4,900. Unwilling to tie up this amount of[20] cash and take the market risk that such a commitment involves, you buy a Call Option for $400 giving[22] you the right to buy 100 shares at 70 within six months.

In that period, suppose Horne and[24] Company climbs to 82. You could exercise your right to buy 100 shares at 70 from the[26] endorser of the Contract and immediately sell it in the open market at 82 for a[28] profit of $1,200 less $400 as the price of the Contract and usual brokerage[30] commissions and taxes. If your judgment is wrong and Horne and Company drops to 50, your loss is limited[32] to $400 as the price of the Call Option; whereas an outright owner of the Stock would have a loss[34] of $2,000 and the possibility of further decline. It is particularly interesting[36] to note that at no time is your possible loss greater than the cost of your Option Contract.

To show the use of[38] a Put Contract for speculation, let us consider the following. You feel that K & L, Inc.,[40] selling at 70 has a good chance of declining to possibly 50 in the next 30 days. You buy a[42] Put Option Contract at 70 good for 30 days for $350. If at any time in the[44] 30-day period K & L, Inc. should decline to 50, you buy 100 shares in the market at[46] 50 and deliver it to the maker of the Put Contract at 70, showing a profit of $2,000[48] less $350, the cost of your Option Contract, less brokerage commissions and taxes. (499)

274

THE ADVERTISING DEPARTMENT

Practically every business advertises in one form or another. Manufacturers of nationally[2] distributed products owe their great mass sales to the powers of advertising. Advertising makes their[4] goods known to the public and stimulates the desire to buy. The advertising department therefore plays an[6] important role in the sales program of a large business concern. For that very reason, it is often organized[8] as a special division of the sales department so that the work of both groups may be synchronized. The[10] advertising department usually plans, writes and designs the sales promotion material used by the firm, such[12] as sales letters, dealer helps, pamphlets, circulars and window displays. However—and this is a point worth[14] remembering—the advertising department does not, usually, prepare the advertising which appears in[16] magazines, newspapers or billboards, or which are heard on radio programs. This advertising is[18] generally prepared by an advertising agency—an organization of expert planners and buyers of[20] advertising, writers, artists, and other people especially trained in the making of advertisements and[22] in placing them in the proper mediums. The advertising department does, however, work closely[24] with the advertising agency, and all the work of the agency is subject to the supervision and[26] approval of the advertising department. All orders for advertising go to the agency and all[28] bills for advertising come from the agency. Thus the large advertiser saves a vast amount of bookkeeping[30] detail and expense and at the same time is assured that his advertising money is being judiciously[32] invested by competent specialists.

Several exceptions should be noted where the advertising[34] agency is not an important factor in the advertising program of a business concern. One is the[36] department store, where advertising must be prepared and published on short notice and where writers must be[38] especially trained in the policies and merchandise of the store. Another exception, obviously, is the[40] catalog mail-order house, where the chief selling effort goes into the making of the catalog, and where the[42] thousands of detailed descriptions and illustrations of merchandise can best be prepared by the company's own[44] especially trained staff. In both the department store and general mail-order house the advertising department looms[46] large in importance and responsibility.

The head of the advertising department is the advertising[48] manager. His job calls for broad experience in all phases of advertising work, as well as the[50] ability to train and direct his assistants in the creation of advertising. He must prepare or[52] assist in the preparation of advertising budgets and is responsible for the results obtained through[54] advertising. His assistants comprise writers, artists, layout experts, and a general office staff of typists, checking[56] clerks and filing clerks.

The Advertising Department of a large concern offers splendid opportunities to[58] learn advertising and selling. Office positions in advertising agencies offer similar opportunities.[60]   (600)

275

SAVING

Wealth that we have created is available for our enjoyment, but it need not be used immediately.[2] If we like, we may save the wealth for use at another time. Some forms of wealth can be saved directly by storing;[4] but most forms are either perishable or bulky, and it is possible then to save wealth only by[6] possessing other forms of wealth, particularly monetary wealth, that can be converted at will into consumable[8] products. Thus one saves primarily by saving money. This process is necessary to the[10] individual in our society, as it is the only way in which he can assure himself of a continued[12] living when he ceases producing as the result of age, illness, or accident, or when he wishes to[14] retire or to take a vacation; and it is the only way in which he can procure luxuries which cost more than[16] his current earnings.

Savings take many forms. Besides the direct hoarding of cash or of imperishable consumer goods,[18] saving may occur through the lending of money and the building up of a credit. This takes the form of bank deposits,[20] or interest-bearing deposits in a savings-bank, or interest-bearing loans to individuals or[22] corporations by notes, mortgages, or bonds. In addition, it is possible to save by buying interests[24] which are less directly convertible into money, such as real estate, buildings, shares in business ventures,[26] and common stocks of corporations. The attraction of any form of saving lies in the possibility[28] of converting the savings into consumer goods, and this is possible because at any time there are other[30] individuals who are willing to accept the saved wealth in exchange for the consumer goods which are constantly[32] being produced. The value of savings, then, depends upon the continuance of our form of society;[34] but within that form its importance to the individual is practically beyond calculation.[36]   (360)

276

MARKET PRICE

When a given commodity changes hands with reasonable frequency, a certain competition is[2] instituted between buyers to find sellers, and between sellers to find buyers. The result is a reduction[4] of the price demanded by the sellers and an increase in the price offered by the buyers until[6] agreement is reached on a compromise or fair price. Thus the price of any article commonly bought and sold is in[8] a sort of equilibrium between two forces, the forces of supply and the forces of demand.

If this[10] equilibrium is in any way disturbed, the nature of the situation immediately produces[12] a new equilibrium. If the supply of an article is increased, or the demand lessened, some[14] sellers will be unable to find buyers and will in consequence reduce their prices. As the price falls fewer[16] sellers are willing to sell and more buyers are willing to buy, until the fall in price produces a new[18] equalization of buying and selling, or of supply and demand, at a new price level lower than that which[20] previously obtained. If the supply of any article is decreased, or the demand increased, some buyers are[22] unable to find sellers, and so increase their bids until the higher bids attract new sellers and repel some[24] of the old buyers to a sufficient extent that a new equilibrium is established.

The law of[26] supply and demand may be represented graphically in this way: on a graph plot a line representing the[28] relationship of price to demand, that is, as the price increases the demand lessens. This line will be straight or[30] curved, depending on the particular commodity selected, and will tend to be tangential to a[32] circle with the origin as center. Plot another line representing the relationship of price to supply,[34] that is, as the price decreases the demand increases. This line also will be indefinite in shape, but it[36] will tend to be at right angles with the previous line. Where the two lines intersect the resulting price can be[38] read from the graph: it is the price at which supply will equal demand.

(394)

277

CREDIT

A bank receives money from its original capital, its conserved profits, and from deposits; it lends that[2] money, plus a good deal more that it does not really possess, to anyone who needs it and who gives evidence[4] of being able to repay. A bank, in the normal course of its operations, will have promised to pay[6] others very much more than it actually possesses. This excess of money loaned over money[8] possessed constitutes an expansion of money in the form of credit, and is possible, just as in the case of[10] governmental issues, because the great majority of these promises to pay will never actually[12] be converted into monetary form.

A bank, for example, establishes a credit of ten thousand dollars in[14] the account of John Smith. Technically, the bank has lent John Smith ten thousand dollars for the needs of his business,[16] and will receive from him interest on that amount. But John Smith may never use more than eight or nine thousand[18] dollars of this credit, and that part which he does use may never leave the bank. He may owe Henry Brown a thousand dollars[20] for merchandise which he has received. This he pays for, ordinarily, not by going to the bank, getting[22] United States currency, and making a payment in cash; but by writing a check for the amount and sending[24] it to his creditor. So Henry Brown has now received a check for one thousand dollars from John Smith. This check he[26] deposits in the bank to his own credit. The bank is now engaged to pay John Smith nine thousand dollars and Henry[28] Brown one thousand dollars; but Henry Brown, in turn, is likely to use this money only in the form of checks, and[30] consequently little if any of the original ten thousand dollar credit of John Smith's may ever leave the bank. Thus a bank having[32] resources of a million dollars might conceivably lend ten million dollars.

But what happens if Henry[34] Brown does not use the same

bank that John Smith uses? Then his check will be deposited in his own bank, which will[36] call upon John Smith's bank for one thousand dollars. A great many such transactions take place every day, and a great many[38] of them normally cancel each other. That is, as various clients of Bank A transfer their funds to[40] clients of Bank B, there are likewise a number of Bank B's depositors who are transferring funds back to Bank A.[42] Only the difference between the two sets of transfers needs to be paid in cash. It is not even necessary[44] to consider the transactions between two banks only. If a number of banks form a group, all the transactions[46] between members of this group can be handled by a common central organization, known as a clearing[48] house, so that only the difference between the incoming and outgoing accounts of each bank need be paid in cash,[50] all the rest being "cleared" by being paired off with an equivalent indebtedness in the reverse direction.[52] Thus we see that of the huge volume of business handled by banks, only an extremely small percentage ever[54] becomes a cash transaction, to be handled by the physical movement of currency, while the great volume[56] of credit swells and flows above the underlying trickle of printed money.   (574)

278

A COMPANY WITH A FUTURE FOR YOU

Nowhere has progress and engineering been a more pronounced factor than in the metal working industry[2] during the past decade. The need for more and better metal products has grown unparalleled, and the W. P. List[4] Company has more than kept pace with this tremendous growth.

Along with this rapid movement has come a need for young,[6] progressive-minded engineers to fill positions of responsibility throughout the Company. As a[8] List engineer you will find an abundance of interesting, stimulating work with a wide diversity[10] of products from high speed can machinery to huge mechanical presses—the same machines that form the bodies on many[12] of the automobiles on the road today.

To better prepare you, as a recent college graduate, for a position[14] of importance with the Company, you will be given the opportunity to grow in industrial[16] know-how and technology through an extensive engineering development training program. This[18] invaluable training will take you through every department of the Company from engineering to accounting and[20] production control and will extend throughout the five major divisions of the Company.

From this comprehensive[22] on-the-job training lasting approximately 60 weeks, you will then be prepared to step into one[24] of many fields such as product engineering, research and development, design or sales engineering.   (249)

279

ABILITY TO WORK WITH OTHERS

Someone has suggested that the chief reason for individual failure in occupations is lack of[2] ability to work well with others. This, far more than competence and skill, accounts for the loss of position with[4] the consequent dislocation and unhappiness. This is the common experience of those who have responsibility[6] for handling personnel at all levels of employment. While that fact is generally recognized, it has not[8] been adequately reflected in educational emphasis. Knowledge, skill in writing and speaking, training[10] for vocations, have been considered the chief objectives of the educational process. Little attention[12] relatively has been given to developing the attitudes and outlook necessary to effective[14] cooperation with others.

The tragedy and waste evident in the career of the maladjusted individual[16] are multiplied a thousandfold when transferred to the group. Labor-management disputes which result in strikes and lockouts[18] are at bottom simply failures in human relations. The interests of both groups are basically the same.[20] Both depend upon the success of the enterprise in which they are engaged, and neither can succeed without the other;[22] yet the waste caused by industrial conflicts is incalculable.

The story of a recent strike and its settlement early in this year through[24] a change in attitude on the part of the president of the company and the chief labor leader is a clear[26] demonstration of the fact that the most aggravated dispute can be settled quickly once the attitude of[28] the contending parties is changed. Apparently the settlement resulted from both parties deciding to try[30] to answer the question "what is right" instead of talking about "who is right."

In a highly industrialized and complex[32] society, a strike in one industry, as all of us know, results in enforced idleness not only of the[34] employees of that industry but of others which depend upon products of the striking company. The result[36] is that a major waste in manpower resources in recent years has resulted from these conflicts. The schools by emphasizing[38] the crucial importance of skill in human relations could have an appreciable effect, in the long run, on[40] domestic conflicts of all kinds; they would thereby add materially to the effective manpower resources of[42] the country.   (412)

280

NUCLEAR POWER DEVELOPMENT PROGRAM OF CONSUMERS PUBLIC POWER DISTRICT, NEBRASKA

Mr. President, I deem it fitting that I make a statement in reference to the Consumers Public[2] Power atomic project in Nebraska. In recent weeks, this matter has been subjected to considerable[4] comment in the news media of the country, in official circles in the Government, by individuals[6] directly connected with the project, and the general public.

The whole field of atomic energy is[8] technical and complex. The peacetime uses of atomic energy are closely related to the[10] defensive uses of atomic energy and, for that reason, certain phases of the whole program have, throughout[12] the years, been in the category of classified material. Sometimes when those of us who are not technically[14] trained in the field discuss matters pertaining thereto, errors are made in terminology and definition.[16] It is not unlikely that some of the comments concerning the controversial legislation which has been[18] before us, and the public comments in reference thereto, have contained some error and misunderstanding.[20]

The measure which was recently passed authorized the appropriation of the full funds for the carrying[22] forward of the Consumers Public Power atomic project. This project has been in the making for some time.[24] Because it was one of the earlier ones, it is in round 1 of the program. Due to the fact that it is in[26] round 1, and for the added reason of the size and competency of the Consumers Public Power District,[28] this project was not put in the category that called for mandatory, direct contracting by the[30] Atomic Energy Commission for the building of the project. This restriction was placed on the later[32] projects sponsored by cooperatives and public bodies which were not placed in round 1, and a number of which[34] are smaller. The Atomic

Energy Commission and the Consumers Public Power District will be free to[36] negotiate a contract and choose the method of construction which is most suitable to both parties. (379)

281

THE SANTA MONICA SHELTERED WORKSHOP

Mr. Speaker, one of the most difficult things in the world to whip is personal discouragement. The conflict[2] is compounded when one suffers a physical handicap which militates against regular employment and[4] takes from one the self-respect which flows from independence. It is a simple matter for one so afflicted to[6] give up the struggle and become a willing victim of what appears to be the inevitability of[8] life's unthinking forces. In such cases, the name of the depressed and unhappy human shows up on the rolls of[10] those receiving public assistance in one form or another. All incentive is lost, as is all desire to seek[12] and achieve the sense of well-being attaching to honest reward for honest labor.

Santa Monica is a[14] booming California city. During the past decade, it has shared in the phenomenal growth which is adding[16] a new permanent resident for California every 55 seconds. Together with its stories of[18] growth, industrial progress, high employment, and general well-being, there were, and are, many good people who[20] for one reason or another found themselves unable to keep the pace required by modern technology and the[22] demands of business and industry. These were the handicapped—those in wheelchairs, in braces, missing one or more[24] members, the blind, the halt. But, one thing they shared in common was the desire to be self-supporting. They wanted an[26] opportunity to learn and to put their sound intelligences to constructive purposes.

They desired deeply[28] to work and to have the quality of their workmanship known and appreciated. Mostly, they had no skills,[30] but in depriving these citizens of sight, or hearing, or a limb, nature had followed the immutable law[32] of compensation. For everything taken from each, something new had been added. The blind developed a[34] deftness of fingers and a keener hearing. The eyes of the deaf were as good, or better, than average. Twisted[36] fingers could be made to perform a useful function, and wheelchairs proved no obstacle to perfect workmanship when the[38] occupant brought determination to the job at hand.

And, out of a welter of disability was[40] born the Santa Monica Sheltered Workshop. In spite of doubts, hardships, heartaches and financial droughts, a few men and[42] women of vision and determination embarked upon what has become a model operation in[44] vocational rehabilitation. What started as a hesitant venture in 1951, has turned out[46] to be, in 1957, a success in every way. Nor, has the success been limited to those who[48] initiated the sheltered workshop, nor to those who have found a new life because of its activities.[50]

The handicapped who comprise the working force of the workshop have demonstrated that physical drawbacks can be[52] overcome. Those who ventured timidly through the office door of the original shack, stayed to gain not only knowledge,[54] but comradeship, confidence, and a new spirit. They defeated not only their own problem, but became, in turn,[56] part of the answer to those who have followed them. The pay check became a reality to many who could[58] previously have hoped for nothing but a meager subsistence check, labeled "Department of Charities, County[60] of Los Angeles."

Out of day-to-day association with others equally handicapped, came a new sense[62] of belonging, a new spirit, a new challenge, and for many, a new life. (635)

282

THE DOMESTIC MINING INDUSTRY

Mr. President, I have been waiting with a great deal of apprehension to see what, if anything, might be done[2] by this Congress to assist the domestic mining industry. Up to this closing day very little has been done.[4]

It has always seemed incongruous to me that while we are spending millions for defense, we have neglected to[6] keep our domestic mining industry healthy. Our defense chain is only as strong as its weakest link, and to[8] date the weakest link has been the sad state of our domestic mining industry. With our imports cut off in time[10] of war, as has been done in the past, and a sick mining industry to provide the needed minerals and[12] metals for a war effort, we are defeating our own purpose.

It is high time that not only our industry[14] leaders but our administration and legislative bodies recognize the drastic need of a strong domestic[16] mining industry.

Something must be done to correct a condition that has been allowed to exist too long, the[18] flooding of our markets with cheap foreign-produced minerals and metals to the detriment of our domestic[20] industry.

The question might be asked as to why these mines are closing all over the country. The answer is simple.[22] First let me say it is not because ore reserves have become exhausted or not because there is no need for the[24] minerals and metals produced. These mines were closed primarily and basically because they cannot produce[26] metal in competition with ores produced by cheap labor in foreign mines. Minerals produced in foreign countries,[28] oftentimes under near slave labor conditions, have flooded our domestic markets to such an extent that the accompanying[30] price drop has forced domestic producers out of business.

A recent article in the Wall Street Journal telling[32] of the cutbacks in the production of one of the country's largest zinc producers, the New Jersey Zinc Co., gives[34] as a reason the "uncontrolled flood of foreign imports," and further quotes company officials as saying:

The[36] excess imports have driven the price down from 13½ to 10 cents a pound within the past 60 days.[38] There can be no improvement in the situation and further production curtailments in the zinc mining and[40] smelting industry are bound to occur unless the United States Government adopts some means of controlling[42] the exploitation of the domestic market by foreign producers.

The article goes on to tell of[44] other closings and cutbacks in the industry.

The situation is serious. When we talk of the mining[46] industry we are not talking of the old prospector and his burro made so popular by western movies[48] and TV classics. We are talking of investments of millions of dollars employing thousands of persons. In May of[50] this year there were 112,200 persons employed by the metal mining industry. This does not include[52] non-metallic mining which employed 117,800 and is also affected to some degree[54] by competition from foreign sources. Two hundred and thirty thousand persons in this country employed in the[56] mining industry and that does not include those employed in smelters and refineries. The jobs of these people[58] and the welfare of their families and the communities in which they live are in jeopardy. It is time that[60] something was done.   (602)

283

THE CITIZEN'S RESPONSIBILITY
IN INTERNATIONAL AFFAIRS

Mr. Speaker:

In speaking to you this afternoon on the citizen's responsibilities in world affairs, I shall be[2] commenting upon problems to which you give a great deal of attention, individually and as an[4] organization. As graduates of American colleges and universities, you have been educated for leadership[6] in a free society. Those of you here from foreign universities represent no less the training for a[8] life of reason, tolerance, and understanding in societies dedicated to the well-being of the[10] individual rather than the glorification of the state.

The interdependence of the modern world[12] has made internationalists of us all. The world has shrunk so much that we do not have much of a choice in[14] the matter. "We must all hang together, or assuredly we shall hang separately." Out of our political,[16] religious, cultural, and historical diversity we seek, and I believe we are finding, a[18] common denominator of values.

Nearly half a century ago Theodore Roosevelt remarked that[20] "The United States of America has not the option as to whether it will or will not play a great part in[22] the world. It must play a great part. All that it can decide is whether it will play that part well or badly."

Today[24] the choice before us is dictated by the need for human survival. With the threat of nuclear war hanging[26] over our heads we have no alternative but to play our part wisely and well. The best insurance that we will[28] do this is a well-informed public opinion carefully following the course of world events.   (294)

284

THE BETTER WAY

Mr. Speaker, during recent weeks, I have listened with interest when some colleagues here in the House have attacked[2] the President for the manner in which he has supported or failed to support various legislative[4] programs before the Congress. They have dwelled particularly on his failure to either pressurize or not[6] pressurize the Members into voting for any one of these programs, a system, which if practiced, could do[8] violence to our form of Government and the constitutional basis of three coequal branches of our[10] Government. It has been my personal feeling that most of these speeches lambasting the President have been[12] motivated by political demagoguery and to cover up for the legislative shortcomings[14] of the Congress.

My views are now reinforced by an excellent editorial appearing in the Wheeling[16] Intelligencer entitled "The Better Way," which places in proper perspective the role of the President[18] and his relationship with the Congress. I commend this editorial to my colleagues, because it clearly[20] delineates what our Founding Fathers had in mind when writing the Constitution to provide for the[22] separation of powers between the executive, legislative, and judicial branches of Government:[24]

The widespread disposition to blame the President for such lack of success as his program has encountered in[26] Congress is an evidence of the degree to which we have accepted distortion of the presidential[28] office.

During the course of a recent press conference, the President voiced disappointment at the refusal[30] of Congress to go along with many of his recommendations. That is only natural. The President[32] believed in his proposals or he would not have made them. What isn't natural is that people would lay the[34] responsibility for this at the President's own door because he didn't take a club to Congress and drive[36] his program through.

An analysis of the Congress-White House relationship by the Pittsburgh Post-Gazette is[38] typical. Acknowledging the political complexion of Congress and the enforced retirement of the President[40] at the conclusion of this term as factors in the situation, the Pittsburgh daily says, nevertheless:[42]

"While these political difficulties have undoubtedly contributed to the President's troubles they are not,[44] it seems to us, the key factor in his defeats. The hard truth is, we fear, that he simply hasn't exerted[46] political leadership of the sort that has characterized some of his predecessors."

Cited as examples[48] of Presidential weakness are his "wavering" on the budget in the face of[50] congressional and public criticism and his "faltering performance over the school bill."

Is it a sign[52] of weakness or strength of character to acknowledge and conform to something so spontaneous and overwhelming[54] as public rejection of a spending policy? As for the school bill, it is difficult to see what more the[56] President could have done. In the eyes of opponents he did entirely too much.

What seems to be overlooked are[58] two basic facts—

First, that a President's belief in and support of a project or a program doesn't[60] necessarily make it good. He could be wrong as this newspaper believes he was, for example, in respect[62] both to the budget and the school-aid bill.

Second, it is the responsibility of Congress, not the President,[64] to levy taxes, appropriate money, enact law. So when the President has made a recommendation[66] and given his reasons for it he has done all that he should do or with propriety can do. By what line of[68] reasoning can we justify the imposition of an Executive's will on the Congress, or the surrender[70] of Congress to his views because they are the President's, or because he is in position to exert[72] political pressure?

There may be those who long for the days of a rubber-stamp Congress. There are others who trace[74] most of the current governmental ills with which we are wrestling to that period and its influence on[76] American life. For its part, the Intelligencer hopes the time never returns when Congress will be a mere[78] puppet of the President.　　　(785)

285

CREATING A CLIMATE OF CONFIDENCE

Public confidence is the one ingredient without which men cannot hope to build a thriving, prosperous, and[2] continuing business. To win and hold public trust in the integrity of any business enterprise starts, of[4] course, with the individual company or organization. But in this highly competitive world, the effort[6] of a single man or company to maintain public confidence and a climate where business can be conducted[8] fairly, honestly and profitably is not enough.

The public, when faced with unfair business tactics, does not[10] always dispose of the situation with: "I should have known better. I'll never go near that place again."

Instead,[12] the entire business or industry is often judged by the actions of a few individuals. Confidence is[14] easily undermined, and responsible organizations as well as the irresponsible feel the loss[16] of income and decrease of profits. In the same manner, a few false ads can destroy trust and belief in all the[18] advertising in a newspaper or over a radio or television station.

Therefore, to offset and[20] to prevent the harm which can be caused by the malpractice of even a single firm, it is necessary to employ[22] collective action—action in which every businessman and organization has a vital stake.

This collective[24] action, because of the complexity of our economic system, cannot be left only to those companies[26] which deal face-to-face with the consumer. While public sentiment is first felt over-the-counter, it does not take long[28] for the chain reaction to reach the service organization, the manufacturer, the producer of raw[30] materials, and, in the long run, all segments of the business community.

When dealing with the public, self-[32]protection requires group participation all the way down the line. It means building confidence with the bricks of[34] honesty and truthfulness so that the business community will flourish in the atmosphere of public support[36] and belief in the American private enterprise system.   (368)

286

TRAINING AND OPPORTUNITIES IN THE
SECRETARIAL OCCUPATIONS

Secretarial training provides complete instruction in the basic skills of Shorthand, Typewriting, Bookkeeping,[2] Business English, and Correspondence. The better trained secretary will also pursue considerable[4] training in such business background subjects as Business Psychology, Secretarial Procedures, Business Law,[6] Taxation and Management.

The secretary is frequently the executive's right hand—accepting many of[8] his responsibilities, presiding over his post when he is absent, is ready at all times to aid in[10] handling special situations, and is in a position to learn many "inside" facts about the business. There is almost[12] no limit to the advancement attainable with ability and proper training. Many of tomorrow's leaders[14] will rise from today's secretaries.

There is a definite shortage of stenographers and secretaries. It is estimated[16] between 4,050 and 5,600 new workers are needed each year as replacements.

Secretarial training[18] is brief when compared to other professions and yet furnishes an enviable opportunity to earn[20] an above-average income while also meeting many people both socially and professionally.

Young[22] men and young women contemplating a secretarial career should select the most comprehensive course that[24] time and money will permit. (245)

287

TRAINING AND OPPORTUNITIES IN THE ACCOUNTING OCCUPATIONS

Probably no other field of employment offers the opportunity for financial remuneration[2] that is afforded the Certified Public Accountant. American business is advancing by leaps and bounds,[4] creating tremendous production and distribution problems. These problems are solved in most instances by[6] scientific and efficient accounting systems.

The field of accounting is broken down into two types of[8] practice, that of private accounting, and that of public accounting. The private accountant is charged with keeping[10] and interpreting the records of his employer. He may be just a bookkeeper, or he may be in charge of[12] the operation of a whole accounting system.

Private accountants in large industries are presented with[14] almost unlimited opportunities for advancement to executive positions. In fact these[16] opportunities are so great that public accountants frequently change to the private accounting field.

The public[18] accountant is an independent accounting expert who makes his services available to those who need[20] them much as a doctor or dentist does. He is called upon to study accounting systems and recommend such changes[22] as may be necessary for the benefit of his client. He frequently installs a completely new[24] system suited to his client's business. He may be an "external" auditor who is employed to verify[26] the records of the private accountant.

Federal and state governments employ thousands of trained accountants.[28] Government pay is usually lower than that of private industry, but other compensating factors cause[30] many to seek civil service employment. (310)

288

RADIO NEWS LETTER

One of the largest automobile manufacturers has just signed a 5½ million dollar network radio[2] deal with a major network. This is the largest radio deal made in 10 years, but perhaps more important, it[4] is undoubtedly the biggest single piece of news since the rise of television. The exact programming[6] hasn't been set, but it will be news and music with personalities. I am certain you will be interested[8] in knowing what it was the agency learned about radio in order for them to recommend this buy. While[10] this was a deal in millions, the important thing to bear in mind is that radio today is ideally[12] suited for medium and small spenders, too.

Let me point out that neither the agency nor the client started[14] out to make a case for radio. The agency was asked to make the best possible recommendation.[16] As a result, there was an extensive 10 month period during which a number of comprehensive media[18] studies were made. As many as 15 to 20 presentations were submitted. At first, radio was almost[20] incidentally a part of these presentations, but as the figures started adding up, as costs were compared,[22] radio started pushing the other media further and further into the background. The agency was[24] the first to be sold on the advisability of using radio. Next came the job of educating[26] the client about the medium. The client had to be schooled on the value of radio, and on its[28] impact as well as the low cost and saturation factors. When all the facts were in, the client made its decision[30] in radio's favor, marking the top allocation for this medium in the company's advertising[32] history.

For radio, the clock had come back to 12, given up for dead with the advent of television[34] it has made a strong comeback on the local level in the past few years. Network radio is once again[36] emerging as a very powerful medium.   (370)

289

YOU AND YOUR PERSONALITY

All of us hear so much spoken about our personality. We have some idea of what is meant by the[2] word, yet few of us would venture to try to give an exact definition. We all know that a person is known by[4] his personality. Of course, everyone wants to have a good, pleasing personality. Everyone wants to[6] be highly thought of by friends and by all with whom he comes in contact.

You might roughly divide personality[8] into two parts: The outward one which we call our appearance, and the inner one which we may call character.[10] Strangers judge you entirely by your appearance. When you come into an office for the first time, you are quickly[12] sized up by the person who is interviewing you. He glances at you and almost unconsciously forms an opinion.[14] Of course it is your hope that this first impression is a good one. Whether it is favorable or not[16] depends upon whether you have the same idea of what an attractive appearance is that your interviewer has.[18] The first thing he looks for is a neat, tidy, harmoniously-groomed person. In dressing for your interview,[20] remember you are going to an office, not to a party, and you should dress accordingly. This generally[22] means simple grooming with coat, dress or suit, hat, shoes, gloves, all to match. Your hair, of course, should be neatly set.

The way you[24] walk makes a strong impression upon a person whose profession it is to interview people. Is your step firm?[26] Does it show a quiet, easy self-confidence? Do you hold your head up, your chin up, your shoulders back? Are you[28] relaxed, and do you have a smile on your face? Is there a minimum of make-up and yet sufficient to show the[30] good lines of your face? Are the seams of your stockings straight in the back? Do you feel that you are making a good impression?[32]

All this an experienced personnel director takes in at one glance. If the firm you are calling upon[34] is a good one, if it is a place where you are anxious to work, then remember that the personnel director[36] is very careful to select only those people who will fit into this organization. When he talks to[38] you, don't interrupt him. Let him finish each statement or question and then answer simply, clearly, and pleasantly.[40]

Keep this in mind if you have made a good first impression: The interviewer wants you to work in his organization.[42] Almost unconsciously, he wants to help you secure the position that you seek. You have won the greater part[44] of the interview with a good impression. Your good personality has carried over to your interviewer[46] so that he becomes your friend. (466)

290

FINANCING AMERICAN IMPORTS

An American merchant wishing to buy goods abroad, say in London, from a firm to whom he was not known, to[2] be paid for on arrival of the goods in the U. S., would have to[4] arrange the business through a banker, because the foreign seller would not ship the goods until he had been paid. There[6] are five steps in the operation as usually conducted:

(1) The American merchant asks his banker[8] to arrange for a credit in London in the merchant's name, that is, he asks the American banker to write[10] to his English branch, or to an English banker, authorizing him to open a credit in his bank for the[12] American merchant, for a certain amount, for a limited time. If the American banker is[14] satisfied as to his customer's financial standing, or if he receives security, he gives the[16] customer a letter of credit which authorizes the London seller to draw a bill on the American[18] merchant for the invoice price and charges and to present this draft for payment to the London banker who is the[20] agent of the American banker. The importer sends this letter of credit to the English firm from whom[22] he orders the goods.

(2) The American banker writes the London banker giving details of the letter of[24] credit and authorizing payment of the seller's draft, provided that the shipping documents, that is, the[26] original invoice, bills of lading and insurance policy, are made out to the order of the shipper[28] and endorsed by him to the American Bank or endorsed in blank.

(3) The English seller packs the goods and delivers[30] them to the steamship company for shipment, and receives a set of bills of lading. He also insures if[32] requested. He then draws a draft on the American merchant for the invoice price of the goods, plus any charges[34] such as freight or insurance which the buyer has agreed to pay. The documentary bill, that is, the draft with[36] the shipping docu-

ments attached, is then presented to the London banker named in the letter of credit.

(4)[38] He pays the amount of the draft and sends it and the documents to the American banker, drawing on him[40] for the amount paid or charging it to his account.

(5) The American banker asks his customer to attend[42] at the bank to "accept" the seller's draft. If the customer gives security, or has good credit with the bank,[44] he will be allowed to take the bills of lading at the time he accepts the draft. Otherwise, the banker will hold[46] the bills of lading and other shipping documents until the customer actually pays the draft. If the[48] goods arrive before payment is made or arranged for, the bank will have them collected and stored in its own name; it can[50] claim delivery by reason of holding the original bill of lading endorsed to it by the shipper.[52]

The bank runs very little risk in these transactions, because it does not pay for the goods abroad until it is[54] satisfied that they have actually been delivered to the steamship company, and it does not part with the[56] shipping documents, which give the right to claim delivery at the destination, until it either receives[58] payment or has the draft accepted by a responsible customer.

The letter of credit gives the banker[60] the right to sell the goods on arrival, in case the importer refuses to accept delivery, and to[62] claim any loss from the importer.   (626)

291

HOW TO STAND

To check up on yourself, stand sideways in front of a full length mirror and scrutinize your outline. Then stand with your[2] back to a wall, heels several inches away from the wall, toes pointed straight ahead, and feet several inches[4] apart. Your hips, shoulders and head should touch the wall. The hips should be pulled back and down as if you were squeezing through a[6] narrow space. Between the small of your back and the wall there should be only the thickness of your hand. Now tilt yourself[8] forward a little from the ankles, and without changing the posture look at yourself in the mirror, comparing[10] your posture now with what it was a few minutes before. To attain this position at other times it is[12] sometimes helpful to imagine that there is a rope attached to the top of your head, constantly pulling you upward[14] and raising your weight off your feet.

The woman who would be graceful should never stand on one foot with the other flung out[16] to the side. Neither should she stand with her feet spread twelve or eighteen inches apart. Probably the most comfortable,[18] and also the most graceful, position is the one in which the feet are placed quite close to each other, with one[20] slightly ahead of the other. Just a little more weight should be put on the forward foot than the back foot. It is[22] interesting to note that character analysts claim that the person who takes this position is one who feels[24] slightly superior, while the person who keeps his feet primly side by side feels ill at ease and inferior.[26] However, whether these emotions are a result or a cause of the foot positions is debatable. The[28] most graceful place for your hands when you are standing is at your sides. For some reason, many women feel awkward with[30] their hands in this position. But your mirror will tell you that it is not as awkward as it feels, and once you get[32] used to it you will feel quite at ease. (327)

292

HOW TO SIT AND RISE

To seat yourself gracefully in a swivel chair at your desk is an extremely difficult job—particularly[2] if it has well oiled rollers. The best you can do is to make sure that the chair does not slide away from you and that[4] you do not fling yourself into it too heavily. But in other types of chairs you should be able to be[6] seated gracefully in this manner: We assume that you have walked up to the chair and now stand facing it, one foot[8] in front of the other, the length of a step apart. Turn your back to the chair by rising slightly on the balls of[10] both feet, without completely raising either foot from the floor. Bend the back knee—the front one will bend too, but the weight[12] is all on the back one—keep the upper part of the body very erect, and lower yourself lightly into the[14] chair. Do not allow your feet to take a side-by-side position when you seat yourself or you will probably find[16] it necessary to take the jack-knife pose which is so awkward. In this pose, the upper part of the body bends[18] far forward, the middle portion juts out over the chair and is laboriously lowered. When you rise from the chair,[20] place one foot in front of the other, and keeping the upper body erect, raise yourself with the leg nearest the[22] chair doing most of the work. To rise without scrambling from the deep easy chairs that one finds in office reception[24] rooms, as well as living rooms, is admittedly difficult. Raise your weight a little and slide forward, using your[26] hands as levers by laying them flat on the seat on each side of you. When you reach the edge of the seat, rise as[28] described above, being careful not to grunt or sigh heavily with the effort.

Incidentally you will look[30] more graceful and tire less quickly if you will pull your chair close to your desk, sit far enough back so that the base of[32] your spine touches the back of the chair, and hold the upper part of the body very erect.   (335)

293

GROOMING

Good grooming is as important to your job and career as the basic skills you bring with you to the office each[2] day, and it would be well for you to read and follow the steps outlined below.

Start a long-range program to[4] establish the foundation for glamour—good health. This means rest, sleep, exercise, proper diet, regular[6] medical and dental checkups, and a reasonable pattern of living. Try to arrange regular sports sessions[8] or dance activities such as weekends of golf, tennis, riding, swimming, perhaps using a lunch hour weekly for[10] bowling. When possible, walk part way to and from work.

Budget your time, set up a tentative schedule to keep yourself[12] and your wardrobe in good order, and keep all necessary equipment handy. It might work best to set aside one[14] evening a week for all beauty and grooming chores, from shampoos and manicures to airing closets, mending[16] lingerie, coffee stains, polishing shoes, and pressing dresses and skirts. Or you may prefer to scatter such tasks through[18] the week just before bedtime or after dinner.

Try to acquire a knack for providing in some degree for the[20] inevitable emergencies. Keep an extra pair of stockings on hand; be sure you can count on at least one[22] wrinkle-resistant dress; for an unexpected date have a flower or special necklace or scarf.

Perk yourself up[24] and give yourself a start by something special in grooming—a good haircut and styling; a professional manicure,[26] pedicure, or facial; a new home permanent if you can't afford a professional one; possibly even[28] a short course by a good beauty salon or cosmetics house in everything from figure control to make-up.[30] You may invest a small fortune in a handsome wardrobe and yet miss being beautifully dressed unless you are[32] perfectly groomed. Basically good grooming depends upon your interest and your constant care.   (358)

294

YOUR LETTERS ARE BEAUTIFUL

Your letters are your company's ambassadors of good will, and just as you judge a business firm by its[2] representatives who call upon you, so other firms judge your company by the letters that you write. Many[4] executives remark that they consider the quality of a secretary's transcript a major factor[6] in evaluating her services. Over and over, men have said: "Please include in your booklet a few hints[8] on making letters beautiful."

Here are some points to watch: See that the letter is properly centered. Make sure that[10] the margins are as even as possible. Learn to use the tabulator for statistical and other work.[12] If you are using a manual typewriter, develop an even touch so that there is a uniform[14] density of printwork.

Your letters are a reflection of your personality, so never release a[16] letter until you have checked it and can say to yourself: "This is a job well done. I can be proud of it."

Even[18] though filing may not be one of your duties, you know its fundamentals. You are a better secretary if[20] you can promptly produce correspondence that your boss needs. Nothing is so irritating as to have to keep[22] a long distance caller waiting while the secretary searches for a letter, or to be told blankly that "the[24] file cannot be found."

The executive welcomes the assurance that you and Webster agree on spelling. An[26] incorrectly spelled or an improperly divided word is a reflection on you, your employer, and your[28] whole organization. It is an inexcusable mistake. To guard against such errors, you keep a[30] dictionary handy. Check any time there is a shade of doubt, and never guess at unfamiliar terms.

Proofread, too,[32] for all other errors before you submit a letter for signature.

(333)

TABULATION
SPECIAL TECHNIQUES
TRANSCRIPTION

PICA AND ELITE

Most typewriters are equipped with either elite or pica type. Elite type, which is the smaller of the two, permits the typing of 12 strokes per inch as compared with 10 strokes per inch for pica. Since most typing is done on paper that is 8½ inches wide, it is possible to type 12 x 8½, or 102 strokes across the line with an elite machine. A machine equipped with pica type, however, allows for only 10 x 8½, or 85 strokes across the line.

Notice the difference in the size of the type on the following lines:

```
ELITE: This is a sample of elite type.
PICA: This is a sample of pica type.
```

To determine whether your machine is equipped with elite or pica type, insert a standard-sized sheet of typing paper into the machine so that the left edge of the paper is at zero on the cylinder scale. Note the position of the right edge of the paper on the scale. The number indicated represents the number of strokes that can be typed across your paper. Therefore, if the right edge of the paper is at 102, you are using a machine that is equipped with elite type—if the right edge is at 85, your machine is equipped with pica type.

Standard single spacing provides six lines of typewriting in a vertical inch. This remains the same for both Elite and Pica type.

INTRODUCTION TO TABULATION

Tabulation is simply the process of typing columns. As a secretary, you will frequently be called upon to type columns either in the body of a letter or in a business form. A knowledge of tabulation techniques will enable you to set up these columns so that they are neatly and attractively placed on the page. Learn the procedures outlined in this section and you will always be proud of your finished work.

When planning the horizontal placement of the tabulation, arrange the material in such a way that it will fall within the space provided for the body of the letter. If possible, it should be indented five or more spaces from each margin. Thus, if a letter is typed with a line of 60 strokes, the width of the tabulation must fall within this definite limit and must not project into the margin area. If the table is so wide that it requires more space than is available between the margins, it should be typed alone on a separate sheet of blank paper and enclosed with the letter (See page 198.)

To separate a table from the body of a letter, allow one blank line above and below the table.

ARRANGING ONE-COLUMN TABLES

A one-column table should be typed so that both the heading and the longest item in the table are centered on the line. Follow this procedure:

1. Center the heading by moving the carriage to the center of the line and backspacing once for every two letters or spaces in the heading.

2. Type the heading all in capital letters.

3. Allow two blank lines below the heading.

4. Select the longest item in the column.

5. Move the carriage to the center of the line and backspace once for every two letters or spaces in the longest item. Set the left margin at this point.

6. Type the column, starting each item at the left margin (except numbers, which are explained below.)

ARRANGING NUMBERS IN COLUMNS

When typing numbers in columns, follow steps one through five as outlined above, but instead of typing the column flush left as in step six, note that:

1. Numbers in columns are typed flush right.

2. Decimal points must line up one below the other.

3. The dollar sign ($) is typed only on the first line and the "total" line, one space to the left of the *longest* line in the column.

When setting the tabulator stop, set it at the point that will require the least amount of back and forward spacing.

$ 43.20	14	Gallons
985.00	7	Cases
72.55	100	Dozen
─────────	23	Gross
$1100.75		

ARRANGING TWO-COLUMN TABLES

As you know, the aim in tabulation is to arrange columns so that they are neatly and attractively spaced. To do this, you can employ either of two commonly-used methods for planning the positioning of columns in table form—the Backspace Method or the Arithmetic Method.

BACKSPACE METHOD

The Backspace Method is simply an extension of the centering technique you have been using, in which a word is centered by backspacing once for every two letters in the word.

Let us assume that we wish to set up our tabulated material as in this example:

WORDS OFTEN MISSPELLED

accommodated	interfere
affect	knowledge
bureaus	maneuver
disappoint	noticeable
develop	occurred
embarrass	parallel
familiar	referred
hygiene	separated

1. Center the heading; then allow two blank lines.

2. Determine the longest word in each column.

   `accommodated    noticeable`

3. Starting at the center of the page, backspace once for each two letters in these words. Do not backspace for an odd letter, and do not allow for any spaces between words.

   `ac  co  mm  od  at  ed  no  ti  ce  ab  le`

4. We must now provide for the spaces between the two columns—the intercolumn. (In this example, we will arbitrarily allow 12 spaces.) To do this, backspace once for each two spaces to be left between columns. (Backspace 6 times for the 12 spaces in this example.) The carriage is now positioned at the starting point for the first column. (If this position falls in the margin area, use a smaller intercolumn.)

5. Set the left margin at the point located in Step 4.

6. We must now determine the position for the second column:

   Strike the space bar once for each letter in the longest word of the first column and once for each space between the columns. Thus, we will space 12 times for the 12 letters in the word *accommodated,* and another 12 times for the spaces to be left between the first and second column. This will give us the starting point for the second column.

7. Set the tabulator stop for the second column. Your machine is now properly set for typing the sample table.

ARRANGING TWO-COLUMN TABLES (Continued)

ARITHMETIC METHOD

We will now outline the steps for planning a tabulation using the Arithmetic Method. So that you may compare procedures, we will use the same problem previously solved by the Backspace Method.

1. On a piece of paper, draw a simple diagram of the problem to be set up, using a bracket to represent each column and a circle within which to write the tabulator stop.

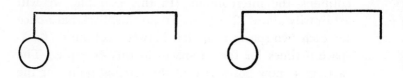

2. Count the number of letters in the *longest* item of each column and place this number in the bracket that represents the column. (In this example: *accommodated*—12, *noticeable*—10.) Also indicate on the diagram the number of spaces to be left between the first and second column—the intercolumn. In this example, we will again use 12 spaces.

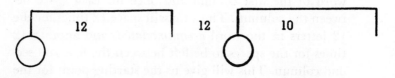

3. Total the number of strokes and spaces for the width of the entire tabulation.

$$12+12+10=34$$

4. If you are using elite type, your page is 102 strokes wide. Therefore, subtract the number of strokes in the tabulation (34) from 102 to determine the number of unused spaces remaining for the right and left margins. (If you are using pica type, subtract 34 from 85.)

102—34=68 spaces available for margins

5. These unused spaces are to be divided equally between the left and right margins—therefore, divide by two.

68÷2=34 spaces for each margin

6. Write this figure on the diagram in the spaces representing the left and right margins.

7. Check your calculations by totaling all the numbers indicated on your diagram. The total should equal the full width of your paper. In this example, which is based on elite type, the total should equal 102.

34+12+12+10+34=102

8. We must now determine the position for the margin and tabulator stops, and set these on the typewriter.

First, start with the left margin—we know this to be 34 and can enter it on the diagram. Then, the position for the second column is determined by adding to the left margin the width of the first column and the intercolumn. (The right margin need not be set.)

190

ARRANGING THREE-OR-MORE-COLUMN TABLES

The procedure to be followed for a table that is composed of three or more columns is much the same as the procedure used for tabulating two columns. The only difference is that the width of more than two columns and intercolumns must be considered when planning the margins and tabulator stops.

GENERAL RULES FOR THE BACKSPACE METHOD

1. Starting at the center of the page, backspace once for each two letters in the longest item in each column.

2. Decide upon the number of spaces to be left between columns. Backspace one-half the total number of spaces to be left between columns. Remember: a table with *four* columns has only *three* intercolumns—always one less than the number of columns. Thus, in a four-column tabulation that is to have 6 spaces between each column (a total of 18 spaces) backspace 9 times.

3. Set left margin at the point reached in Step 2.

4. To determine the position of each column, space forward *once* for each letter in the longest word in the column and *once* for each space between columns. Having set the tabulator stop at this point, proceed in the same way to locate the other stops.

GENERAL RULES FOR THE ARITHMETIC METHOD

1. Draw a diagram of the problem using a bracket to represent each column.

2. Count the number of letters in the longest item in each column and enter it on the diagram.

3. Decide upon the number of intercolumn spaces and enter these on the diagram.

4. Total the number of strokes and spaces used for the entire width of the table and subtract this figure from the spaces available across the page—102 for elite, 85 for pica.

5. Determine the number of spaces for the left and right margins by dividing this number by two. Enter this figure in the diagram in the spaces representing the margins.

6. Check your calculation by totaling all the numbers indicated on your diagram. The total should equal the full width of your paper—102 for elite, 85 for pica.

7. Set your left margin as indicated on the diagram. Locate the tabulator stop for the second column by adding together the left margin setting, the width of the first column, and the intercolumn. To locate the tabulator stop for the third column, add to the tabulor stop for the second column the width of the second column and intercolumn.

   In practice, the tabulator stop for any column is merely the total of all the figures to the left of the column.

MORE ABOUT HEADINGS

The headings that are typed above a tabulation may be divided into three general groups:

1. Main heading—the title of the table.
2. Secondary heading—the subheading.
3. Column heading—the title of each column.

Generally, tabulations in the body of a letter will only require column headings. Tables that require multiple headings most often are complex enough to be typed on a separate sheet of paper.

ACHIEVEMENT TESTS			MAIN HEADING } 2 BLANK LINES
Friday, September 10, 19—			SECONDARY HEADING } 2 BLANK LINES
Subject	Time	Room	COLUMN HEADINGS } 1 BLANK LINE
Accounting	9:45	403	FIRST LINE OF COLUMN
Bookkeeping	11:30	315	
Business English	1:30	209	
Filing I	2:00	217	
Filing II	10:30	412	
General Business	1:00	303	
Merchandising	9:00	317	
Stenography I	10:00	605	
Stenography II	2:00	306	
Typewriting	2:30	334	

MAIN HEADING

1. Type the main heading all in capital letters.
2. Center it above the table.
3. Allow two blank lines below the main heading.
4. A main heading that extends beyond the width of the table should be divided into two lines. In such cases, make the first line a little longer than the second.

SECONDARY HEADING

1. Capitalize the first letter of each word unless it is a preposition, article, or conjunction. If such a word begins the heading, however, it should be capitalized.

2. Center the secondary heading above the table.

3. Allow two blank lines below it.

COLUMN HEADINGS

1. Capitalize the first letter of each word unless it is a preposition, article, or conjunction. If such a word begins the heading, however, it should be capitalized.

2. Center the column heading above its column (see explanation on next page). When the heading of a column is longer than the longest item in the body of the column, use the heading to determine the tabular setting for the column. (After the heading has been typed, however, the tabulator stop that was set for it should be cleared and a new one set to center the body of the column under the heading.)

3. If a column heading contains several words, it should be divided into two or more lines, each centered above the column.

4. Underscore the last line of the column heading, extending the underscore only to the width of the column heading, even if the column is wider than the heading.

Hospital	Number of Patients	Number of Doctors in Attendance

5. Allow one blank line before typing the table.

CENTERING COLUMN HEADINGS

The heading of a column should be centered above the column. First locate the center point of the column. Finding this center point may be done by using either the backspace or the arithmetic method.

BACKSPACE METHOD

1. Move the carriage to the beginning of the column.
2. Tap the space bar once for each two letters in the longest word in the column. Do not space for an odd letter. This will move your carriage to the midpoint of the column.
3. Backspace once for each two letters in the heading that is to appear above the column. Then type the heading.

ARITHMETIC METHOD

The figures used in this example were obtained from the problem on pages 186-189.

1. Divide the width of a column by 2. Drop any fraction.

34 | 12÷2=6 | 12 | 10÷2=5 | 34

(34)   (58)

2. Add the above result to the beginning point of each column to get the center point of the column.

34+6=(40)   58+5=(63)

34 | 12÷2=6 | 12 | 10÷2=5 | 34

(34)   (58)

3. Using the backspace method, center each heading above its column.

BRACED HEADINGS

A braced heading is one that identifies more than one column.

1. Capitalize the first letter of each word unless it is a preposition, article, or a conjunction. If such a word begins the heading, however, it should be capitalized.

2. The braced heading is to be centered over the entire space that it braces.

3. Underscore the braced heading, extending the underscore only to the edges of the *headings* that it braces, even if the columns extend beyond their headings.

4. Allow one blank line between the braced heading and the column headings.

5. In practice, leave space for the braced heading, but do not type it until the column headings have been typed. After typing the column headings, roll the cylinder back and type the braced heading.

	Salaries	
Department	Day	Evening
Accounting	$13,478	$4,220
Office	8,457	4,375
Sales	84,320	2,405
Shipping	7,885	1,600

FOOTNOTES

Footnotes are used to clarify or enlarge on an item listed in tabulated material. Follow these rules when including a footnote in a tabulation:

1. Allow at least one blank line between the table and the footnote.

2. A short footnote is centered under the tabulation. If it requires more than one line, however, it should be typed as a single-spaced paragraph no wider than the table.

MIDWINTER FURNITURE SALE

Open—Stock Dining Room*

Piece	Regular Price	Sale Price
**Shield—back Side Chair	$ 29.50	$ 24.50
Breakfront	186.00	173.00
Credenza	193.00	178.00

*Mahogany-finished hardwood
**Available in other finishes

FOOTNOTES WITH ASTERISKS

3. Use an asterisk to indicate one or two footnotes, but use raised letters or raised numerals if there are more than two footnotes. (See page 217 for instructions on typing raised characters.)

4. In a heading, any identifying mark is typed after the heading.

5. In a column, asterisks are typed on the straight side of the column; numbers or letters are typed after the item.

6. In the footnote, the identifying mark precedes the footnote.

7. Do not include the asterisks or raised characters in your calculations when determining tabulator stops.

MIDWINTER FURNITURE SALE

Open-Stock Dining Room[1]

Piece	Regular Price	Sale Price
Shield-back Side Chair[2]	$ 29.50	$ 24.50
Breakfront	186.00	173.00
Credenza[3]	193.00	178.00

[1]Mahogany-finished hardwood
[2]Available in other finishes
[3]Mahogany front

FOOTNOTES WITH NUMERALS

PLACEMENT OF INSIDE ADDRESS

In planning the vertical placement for the inside address of a letter that contains a table, it is necessary to allow for the number of lines that the table will occupy. In order to make the adjustment for these additional lines, proceed as follows:

1. Determine the number of words in the body of the letter—excluding the tabulation.

2. Count the number of lines that the full table will occupy, remembering to allow one blank line above and below the tabulation to separate it from the body of the letter.

3. Multiply the number of lines in the tabulation by 10.

4. Add this number to the total number of words in the body of the letter. Using this new total, refer to the chart on page 238 to determine the vertical placement of the inside address.

TABULATING ON A BLANK PAGE

When a table is very long, complicated, or wider than the body of the letter, it should be typed on a separate blank sheet of paper and enclosed with the letter. In this case, short tables may be double spaced. (See sample on page 192.)

In setting up material on a blank page, your objective is to center the material in such a way that the margins at the top and bottom of the page will be the same. Following the procedure outlined below will enable you to accomplish this.

1. Count the number of lines that the material will occupy. Take into consideration all extra lines required for headings or double spacing.

2. Since there are 6 typewritten lines per inch (with both pica and elite type), an 8½ x 11-inch page will contain 66 lines from top to bottom. Therefore subtract from 66 the number of lines needed for the tabulation to determine the total number of lines available for the top and bottom margins.

3. Divide this total number of lines by 2 to determine the number of lines to allow for the top margin.

This Set of Books Is
VALUABLE
TO YOU

You must present this set of books along with the International Registration Form (Page 116 of Book 1), properly validated, when you apply for YOUR LIFETIME PRIVILEGES.

Do not lend or sell these books to anyone. You must have them when you apply for your privileges or you LOSE ALL PRIVILEGES.

You should receive your validated International Registration Form from our home office in New York within 60 days after you start your SPEEDWRITING Course.

If you do not receive your validated International Registration Form, please notify:

Speedwriting Publishing Co., Inc.
55 West 42nd Street
New York 36, New York

MAINTAINING THE RIGHT-HAND MARGIN

When transcribing your shorthand notes, it will be necessary for you to decide where to end each typewritten line in order to maintain a reasonably straight right-hand margin.

The bell on your typewriter will serve to warn you that six or eight strokes may be typed before the carriage locks against the right margin. Thus, as you type, listen for the sound of the bell. When you hear it, finish the word you are typing—if it is not too long—and throw your carriage without taking your eyes from your notes.

If typing only two or three strokes beyond the margin will permit you to complete the word, strike the margin release when the carriage locks at the margin and insert these extra letters. However, if the word you are typing is too long for your line of type, divide it properly as explained below, and continue the word on the next line.

WORD DIVISION

The trend in letter writing today is to avoid the use of word divisions whenever possible. Therefore, the guiding rule of every typist should be to divide words only when it is absolutely necessary to do so in order to maintain a *reasonably* straight right margin. A line of type that is five spaces shorter than the margin or three spaces longer is acceptable.

Learn the following rules before you transcribe your notes:

1. When dividing a word, the hyphen should be typed at the end of the first line.

2. Do not divide a proper noun, a contraction, an abbreviation, or a number.

3. If possible, do not divide a word if it is the last word of a paragraph or a page.

4. Do not end more than two successive lines with a divided word.

5. Do not divide a one-syllable word or a word of less than five letters.

```
where        please        talked
think        through       shipped
```

6. Carry over at least three or more letters.

Correct:	shortly	Incorrect:	short-ly
	lux-ury		luxu-ry
	con-sumer		consum-er

7. Divide words only between syllables. However, do not divide a word in such a way that a single letter is separated from the remainder of the word. (If you are in doubt as to the proper syllabication of a word, take the time to consult your dictionary.)

Correct:	con-tain	Incorrect:	e-lated
	trans-fer		a-mong
	edu-cates		radi-o
	con-di-tion		o-blige

8. Divide compound words only at the point where the hyphen occurs.

```
self-control        above-mentioned
```

9. As a general rule, divide words between double letters unless the word is derived from one that ends in a double letter (sma*ll*). In the latter case, the word is divided after the root word.

```
small-est        rub-ber
woo-ing          excel-lence
stuff-ing        win-ning
```

Remember—When in doubt, consult the dictionary.

RULES FOR CAPITALIZATION

The following are the most important rules governing the capitalization of words. You should use a capital letter for:

1. The first word in a sentence.

   ```
   Send it to them now.
   ```

2. A proper name or a derivative from a proper name.

   ```
   John Smith     America     American
   ```

3. A noun that is part of the name of a *specific* product, geographical location, hotel, highway, etc.

   ```
   The best fan is the Arctic Fan.
   The Mississippi River is the longest river
   in America.
   The finest hotel is the Hotel Sands.
   ```

4. The title of a person when it appears *directly* before or after the name of the title-holder. There is some disagreement about whether the title of a person should be capitalized when his name does not appear in a sentence. The preferred business practice is to capitalize such titles, especially the title of high-ranking officers. After all, you express your respect for a person when you capitalize his title.

   ```
   Send the message to John Johnson, Presi-
   dent of the Acme Steel Company.
   The Sales Manager called the meeting to
   order.
   BUT: Do you know who is the sales manager
   of the Ajax Company?
   ```

5. The name of a point on the compass when it refers to a specific geographical area, but NOT when it refers to a direction.

   `The West is less populated than those areas east of the Mississippi.`

6. The name of a month or a day, but NOT of a season.

   `The first day of spring will be Tuesday, March 21.`

7. Each word in the title of a work of art or literature, except prepositions, conjunctions, and articles. However, the first word is *always* capitalized.

   `Have you read "How to Win Friends and Influence People"?`

8. The first word in a direct quotation that starts a complete sentence.

   `"This job," he said, "must be improved upon."`

9. A noun or pronoun that refers to God or specific holy books.

   `In the Bible we are told that God created the world in six days and that He rested on the seventh day.`

CARBON COPIES

It is customary to make a carbon copy of every letter or form that is typed in a business office. The number of copies required will depend upon the procedures followed by the organization. As a general rule, at least one carbon copy will be made and kept in the company files.

Carbon copies of business letters are never typed on letter-head stationery. Instead, a blank sheet (generally inexpensive yellow paper or onionskin) is used. Carbon copies of business forms—such as invoices or statements—are typed on printed forms similar to the original.

Notice that there is a dull side and a glossy side to a sheet of carbon paper. (See illustrations.) It is the glossy side that prints. Therefore, the glossy side is placed *against* the sheet on which the carbon copy is to be made.

To prepare your paper for insertion into the machine:

1. Lay the paper to be used for the carbon copy on your desk. Place the carbon paper over it, with the glossy side down.

2. On top of these sheets, place the letterhead, face up. Note in the lower left illustration the arrangement for an original and two copies.

3. Place the sheets in position for insertion with the printed letterhead resting against the paper table.

4. Check for the proper arrangement of the carbon paper by making sure that its glossy side faces you as the papers are being inserted behind the cylinder.

5. Insert the papers.

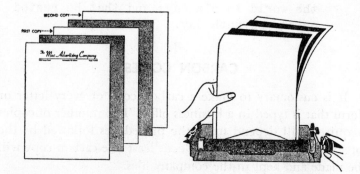

6. When it is necessary to insert a thick pack of several sheets into the machine, the sheets may be kept in alignment during insertion by placing a folded piece of paper, or the flap of an envelope, over the top of the sheets. (See illustration at the lower right corner of the preceding page.)

For erasing carbon copies, see the following page.

ERASING

Accurate typing is a prerequisite for a capable secretary. The most experienced secretary, however, will occasionally make an error when typing, and it is therefore essential to learn the proper methods for correcting these mistakes.

If you must erase an error, follow these steps so as to avoid the necessity of retyping the letter completely:

1. Move the carriage to either the left or the right, past the margin stops, so that the erasure particles will not drop into the "well" or basket of the machine and clog the keys.
2. Raise the paper bail out of the way.

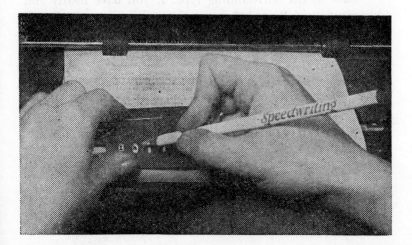

3. If the correction is to be made on the upper two-thirds of the page, turn the paper up to a convenient position. If the correction is to be made on the lower part of the page, turn the cylinder backward so as not to disturb the alignment of the typing line.

4. Use an eraser shield to protect the letters surrounding the one to be corrected. These shields, made either of metal, paper, or celluloid, are perforated in such a way that the perforations can be placed over the letters to be corrected thus avoiding any unintentional erasing of the letters around it.

5. Proper erasing technique requires a *light,* short, downward stroke. Do not "scrub" or you will suddenly find a hole in your paper. Using a clean eraser, stroke downward lightly. Examine your progress after each stroke of the eraser. The trick is to erase as *little* as possible. When the erasure is complete, blow any erasure crumbs off the page or typewriter.

6. Return the carriage to the proper position and *lightly* strike the correct letter. Backspace, and strike it *lightly* again, continuing this process until the correction is as dark as the surrounding type. If you have neatly and carefully followed these steps, your erasure will not be noticed.

ERASING CARBON COPIES

When erasing an original letter with one or more carbon copies, the general steps outlined on the previous page must be supplemented by the following:

1. Before making the erasure, insert a *stiff* card *immediately* behind the spot where the correction is to be made. Doing this will prevent the pressure used in erasing from smudging the other copies. After each correction is made, remove the card and place it behind the next copy to be erased.

2. Use a hard eraser on the original copy and a soft eraser for correcting carbon copies. Make certain the eraser is clean before attempting to make a correction with it.

3. To darken a carbon correction after erasing, set the ribbon control lever in stencil position and firmly type over the original copy.

SQUEEZING AND EXPANDING

HALF-SPACE METHOD

Errors resulting from the insertion or omission of a single letter or space can be corrected by a method known as "half-spacing." This method takes advantage of the fact that the space bar on most typewriters moves the carriage forward in two half-space movements—one half space when the bar is depressed and another half space when the bar is released. Thus, by properly operating the space bar it is possible to insert or delete extra letters by increasing or decreasing the *space between words* by a half space.

To check your machine for half-spacing, press down on the space bar and then release it. If the carriage moved twice—both when you depressed the bar and when you released it—you may use the following method for the insertion of an omitted letter. If it moved only once, you must use the back-space method explained on the second following page.

To *insert* a single letter with the half-space method:

Example: They se the typewriter.   (*se,* instead of *see*)

1. Erase the entire word that is to be corrected. (In this example, erase *se.*)

2. Move the carriage to the space *after* the previous word. (In this example, move the carriage to the space after *they.*)

3. Depress the space bar (this moves the carriage a half space) and, *keeping the space bar in a depressed position,* type the first letter of the corrected word. (In this example, strike *"s."*)

4. Release the space bar and depress it again and, *while the space bar is depressed,* strike the second letter (*e*) of the word that is being corrected. Continue in this way until the last letter has been inserted. Remember—the space bar must be in the depressed position while each letter is being inserted.

    Result: They see the typewriter.

To *eliminate* an unnecessary letter with the half-space method:

Example: Tell them about it.   (Change *them* to *her.*)

1. Erase the entire word that is to be corrected—*them.*

2. Move carriage to where the first letter had been. (In this example, move carriage to the original *"t"* position.)

3. Depress the space bar and, *while the space bar is depressed,* strike the first letter of the correct word. (In this example, strike *"h."*)

4. Release the space bar and depress it again for the insertion of the second letter (*e*). Continue in this way until the last letter has been inserted.

    Result: Tell her about it.

BACKSPACE METHOD

For machines that do not half-space, use the following methods to insert or delete letters:

1. Erase the entire word that is to be corrected.

2. Move the carriage to where the *first* letter of the original word had been.

3. To *insert* a single letter, space *once* . . . To *delete* a single letter, space *twice* . . . and then *fully* depress the backspace key. Keeping it depressed, strike the first letter of the word that is to be inserted.

4. Release the backspace key and space once. Depress the backspace key again and, *while it is depressed,* insert the next letter.

5. Release the backspace key and repeat Step 4 until the entire word has been corrected.

RULES FOR TYPING NUMBERS

WHEN TO SPELL OUT NUMBERS AND WHEN TO USE FIGURES

1. Spell out whole numbers from one through ten. Use figures above ten.

```
We sent four packages.
He received ten letters.
They ordered 11 sets of books.
This mailing consisted of 10,000 letters.
```

2. Spell out numbers that begin a sentence, no matter how large. (When a long number begins a sentence, it is often better to rearrange the sentence.)

```
Two hundred twenty-eight men applied for
the job.
The job was applied for by 228 men.
```

3. Generally spell out approximate numbers that have been rounded out.

```
About three hundred men applied for the
job.
```

4. Ordinal numbers are "first," "second," "third," etc. Spell out ordinal numbers from *first* through *tenth*. Use figures for *11th* and above.

```
This is my fourth visit to your city.
He succeeded on the 11th attempt.
This is my 25th crossing.
```

5. When two numbers appear one after the other, spell out the smaller number and express the larger number in figures. This prevents confusion.

```
The purchasing department ordered eleven
55-gallon drums.
We need 11 three-cent stamps.
```

6. Use figures in all statistical typing and tabulation, and in all business forms.

```
4 cartons      No. 10 envelopes
3 boxes        8" x 10" letterheads
12 cartons     3" x 5" index cards
```

7. When a series of numbers includes numbers both above and below ten, use figures for all the numbers.

```
We ordered 8 boxes of paper, 12 boxes of
envelopes, and 20 cartons of index cards.
```

HYPHENATING SPELLED-OUT NUMBERS

1. Hyphenate spelled-out numbers from twenty-one through ninety-nine.

```
Twenty-one
Forty-six
Ninety-nine
```

2. Do not hyphenate before the words *hundred, thousand,* etc. (Note: The *and* may be omitted.)

```
One hundred and twenty-one
One thousand three hundred forty-six
Seventy-six thousand four hundred and
ninety-nine
```

3. When a number appears as a modifier directly *before* a noun, the entire number should be hyphenated.

```
We are planning a six-thousand mile trip.
It will be a 12-page booklet.
```

WRITING FIGURES

1. Figures from 1 to 1000 are written without commas.

```
32              932             1000
```

2. Figures above 1000 are generally written with commas to separate every three digits. This permits ease of reading. Leave no space before or after the comma.

```
1,001           1,426           227,320
```

3. Below 10,000 you may omit the commas from numbers rounded out to the nearest hundred; above 10,000, the comma must be included.

```
1100            1,101           10,000
5200            5,274           10,100
9900            9,999           23,500
```

4. When two figures appear one after the other, separate them by a comma. Skip a space after the comma.

```
Of 1700, 23 were rejected.
```

5. Form the plural of a figure by adding an apostrophe followed by the letter **s** ('s). If a number is spelled out, just add the letter **s**.

```
8's and 9's
eights and nines
1900's
```

FRACTIONS

There are two kinds of typewritten fractions—those that are on the keyboard ($\frac{1}{2}$) and those that are "made" by using the diagonal (1/19). Note that there is no space before or after the diagonal.

1. Use figures for all mixed numbers. With a "keyboard" fraction, no space is left between the whole number and the fraction. With a "made" fraction, one space is left.

```
2½          2 5/16
4¼          18 4/100
```

2. Do not use a "keyboard" fraction ($\frac{1}{2}$) in the same sentence with a "made" fraction (1/8).

```
      The lot measures 84 1/2 by 26 1/8 feet.
NOT:  The lot measures 84½ by 26 1/8 feet.
```

3. Spell out all isolated fractions. Generally, hyphenate such a fraction.

```
The job is two-thirds completed.
Asphalt was used for four-tenths of a
mile.
```

DECIMALS

1. A period is used to express a decimal point. Do not skip a space before or after the period.

   1.06   12.412   128.627

2. Do not use commas in the decimal part of a number.

   1.08
   47.62432
   2,974.4216

ROMAN NUMERALS

Roman numerals are easily typed by using capital letters. For numbers over 5,000, note how the *V* or *M* is overscored by using the underscore key.

1	I	11	XI	30	XXX	400	CD
2	II	12	XII	40	XL	500	D
3	III	13	XIII	50	L	600	DC
4	IV	14	XIV	60	LX	700	DCC
5	V	15	XV	70	LXX	900	CM
6	VI	16	XVI	80	LXXX	1000	M
7	VII	17	XVII	90	XC	1500	MD
8	VIII	18	XVIII	100	C	2000	MM
9	IX	19	XIX	200	CC	5000	$\overline{V}$
10	X	20	XX	300	CCC	1,000,000	$\overline{M}$

   1800   MDCCC
   1920   MCMXX
   1755   MDCCLV

1. Use of Roman numerals:

   Henry VIII   John Astor III   Chapter XI

2. When writing a series of Roman numerals, leave an extra space after each comma:

   Volumes X, XII, XX, XXV

REFERENCE CHART FOR THE USE OF NUMBERS

ADDRESS	See pages 226 and 228.	
AGE	Spell out an age stated in years. Use figures for an age that includes months and days. Omit commas between the years, months, and days.	I am eighteen. I am 18 years 4 months and 27 days old.
DATES	Use figures except in extremely formal documents. Use -st, -nd, -rd, -th in a date *only* when the day is written before the month. The year may be abbreviated by using an apostrophe for the century.	August 6, 19— the 6th of August Class of '61 the blizzard of '88
DIMENSIONS FEET INCHES WEIGHTS DISTANCE	Use figures for dimensions. In technical material, use the apostrophe (') to represent feet, and quotation marks (") to represent inches. Do not space between the number and mark. Note use of number sign (#) for pounds.	4 by 6 feet 4' x 6' 4 feet 6 inches 4'6" 6 lbs. 6# 3 miles
LEGAL DOCUMENTS	At one time, numbers were spelled out, followed by the figure in parentheses. Modern practice tends toward the use of figures only.	We agree to sell thirty-three (33) acres. We agree to sell 33 acres.

Category	Rule	Example
MONEY	Use figures, except in extremely formal legal documents. Do not space after the dollar sign.	$12.73 $8.05 $12 $3.45 list, $3.00 net
	Omit the decimal point and ciphers for even amounts (except in checks or in a series that contains an uneven amount).	
	For amounts under $1, use the cent sign (¢) only in invoices, etc.	4 @ 8¢ We paid 8 cents.
PERCENTAGES	Use figures to express percentages. Percent may be written as one word or as two.	12 percent 12 per cent 12%
	Use the percentage sign (%) only in business forms and statistical work. Do not space before the percentage sign.	
REFERENCE NUMBERS	Use figures for reference numbers that identify a model, style, policy, invoice, purchase order, page, volume, etc. Generally omit all commas in such numbers.	Model #23546 Policy No. S98467 Invoice 20741
	Common nouns, such as model or chapter, should be capitalized when used before reference numbers.	Chapter 7 Lesson III Room 2
TIME	Spell out the hour with o'clock.	four o'clock
	Use figures with a.m. and p.m. Either lower case or capital letters may be used. Do not space after *a.* or *p.*	4 a.m.
	Use a colon to separate hours from minutes and minutes from seconds.	4:03 P.M. 4:03:26

CHARACTERS NOT ON THE KEYBOARD

!	EXCLAMATION POINT	Type the apostrophe, backspace, and type the period On some machines, it is possible to hold down the space bar with the left thumb, depress the shift key with the left hand, and type the apostrophe and then the period without backspacing.	Indeed! Yes!
=	EQUAL	Strike the hyphen, backspace, depress the shift key *slightly* and type the hyphen a second time.	12 x 12 = 144
÷	DIVIDE	Strike the hyphen, backspace, and strike the colon.	100 ÷ 2 = 50
—	SUBTRACT	Type the hyphen with a space before and after it.	144 - 44 = 100
X	MULTIPLY	Strike the small letter "x" with a space before and after.	16 x 5 = 80
°	DEGREE	Use ratchet release, turn cylinder toward you one-half space and strike the small letter "o" without spacing after the number. Return ratchet release to normal typing position and turn cylinder back to original line of typing.	38° North
'	MINUTES OR FEET	Strike the apostrophe without spacing after the number.	
"	SECONDS OR INCHES	Strike the quotation marks without spacing after the number.	6'4" long

217

said[2]	RAISED FIGURES	Use ratchet release, turn cylinder toward you one-half space and insert the desired number or letter. Return ratchet release to normal typing position and turn cylinder back to original line of typing. The bottom of the raised number or letter should be on a line with the top of a lower case letter.	book[2] had merit.
H_2O	SUBNUMERALS	Use ratchet release, turn cylinder away from you one-half space and insert the desired number. Return ratchet release to normal typing position and turn cylinder back to original line of typing. A subnumeral may also be inserted by depressing the shift key halfway before striking the desired number.	H_2SO_4
c/o	CARE OF	Strike the small letter "c", the diagonal, and the small letter "o".	c/o Postmaster
--	DASH	Strike the hyphen twice, without spacing before or after it. The dash may also be typed by striking the hyphen once, spacing both before and after it.	Now--not later. Now - not later.
+	PLUS SIGN	Type the hyphen, backspace, use the ratchet release to roll the paper slightly upward, and strike the apostrophe repeatedly while returning the roller.	18 + 20 = 38
7/8	FRACTIONS	See page 212.	
III	ROMAN NUMERALS	See page 213.	

215

PROPER SPACING FOR MARKS OF PUNCTUATION AND CHARACTERS

Mark	Rule	Example
.	Space twice after a period at the end of a sentence. Space once after a period at the end of an abbreviation.	Order now. It's not too late. Mr. C. L. Bradley
?	Space twice after a question mark	Did you go? No.
!	Space twice after an exclamation point.	No! Yes! Not really!
:	Space twice after a colon.	as follows: bills, clips, and pencils.
,	Space once after a comma.	Invoices, bills, and statements.
;	Space once after a semicolon.	All orders must be entered; all bills must be paid.
"	No space between opening quotation marks and the first word of the quoted material. Space once after the closing marks if they are not at the end of a sentence.	She marked "paid" on the bill.

"	A period or a comma is typed *before* the quotation marks. If the quoted material is a question or an exclamation, but the rest of the sentence is not, type the question mark or exclamation point *inside* the quotation marks. If the entire sentence is a question or an exclamation, type the question mark or exclamation point *outside* the quotation marks. The semicolon, colon, and dash are always typed outside the quotation marks.	"The book," she said, "is very interesting." I heard her ask, "Where are you going?" The man said, "What a beautiful sight!" Who purchased "Typing Techniques"? The following are considered "standard equipment":
—	When using two hyphens to indicate a dash, do not space before, between, or after the hyphens. When a single hyphen is used as a *dash*, space once before and after it.	He came today—didn't you meet him? He came today -- didn't you see him?
-	No space before or after the hyphen.	A first-class job. Second-hand car.

PROPER SPACING FOR MARKS OF PUNCTUATION AND CHARACTERS (Continued)

	Rule	Example
'	No space before or after an apostrophe.	I can't find Mary's record. I'll check it at two o'clock.
( )	Space once before typing the opening parenthesis and once after typing the closing parenthesis, but do not space between the parentheses and the words they enclose.	In the illustration given (see below) the purpose is made clear.
	Type the comma, semicolon, colon, and dash after the closing parenthesis.	Although we are not satisfied with our order (there are too many broken pieces), we are paying the bill.
	A period, question mark, or exclamation point is typed outside the parentheses when it punctuates the entire sentence. These marks of punctuation are placed inside the parentheses when they punctuate the enclosed material.	They met at the Waldorf (Hotel). We have waited 30 days (doesn't it seem longer?) for the package.

Symbol	Rule	Example
&	One space before and after the ampersand.	Mark & Sons
#	Do not space between the number sign and the number it identifies.	Style #34, Bill #45
$	No space between the dollar sign and the number it identifies.	We have a bill for $35.
%	No space between the percent sign and the number it identifies.	A discount of 18%.
*	Often used to refer to a footnote. Do not space between the asterisk and the word that precedes it.	This article* appeared two months ago.
@	One space before and after the "at" sign.	4 @ $3.50
¢	Do not space between the cent sign and the number it identifies.	15 lbs @ 18¢
/	When used to express a fraction, do not space between the numbers of the fraction and the diagonal.	A total of 4 3/8 inches.

REINSERTING PAPER

It is possible to remove paper from the machine and then reinsert it in such a way that its removal cannot be detected. The ability to perform this technique thus enables the secretary to either continue with a letter that was removed before it was finished or correct an error that was not noticed while the paper was in its original typing position.

To reinsert your paper into the machine, follow these instructions carefully:

1. Insert paper to the approximate position desired.

2. Make certain the card holders are lowered.

3. Using the paper release, straighten the paper, meanwhile shifting it until an "*i*" or "*l*" in your copy is in perfect alignment with the calibration marks on the alignment scale.

4. Using the variable line spacer, move the cylinder until the original line of typing is even with the top of the alignment bar.

5. Check the accuracy of your reinsertion by putting the ribbon selector in stencil position and type over one of the original letters. The faint impression that results will indicate whether further adjustments are necessary.

6. When the strikeover indicates perfect alignment, return the ribbon selector to normal position and continue typing.

If you are reinserting the paper to make a correction, do not try to correct both the original and carbon copies at the same time. Instead, insert each sheet separately and make the correction.

TYPING ON RULED LINES

To type on a ruled line, use the variable line spacer when rolling the paper to the correct typing position. This correct position will be found by rolling the cylinder until the ruled line is slightly below the alignment bar. In this position, the letters to be typed will not cross the ruled line or be too far above it. After a printed heading, allow two blank *spaces*.

Example: Proper typing on a ruled line.

INTRODUCTION TO THE BUSINESS LETTER

The letters that a firm sends are often the only contact between the firm and its customers. It is essential, therefore, that these letters create a favorable impression. A letter that is attractive in appearance is, in a sense, a good-will ambassador, and your ability to type an attractive letter is your "hallmark" as an efficient, capable typist or secretary.

PARTS OF THE BUSINESS LETTER

A business letter generally contains the following parts:

Letterhead	Complimentary close
Date line	Company name
Inside address	Dictator's name and/or title
Salutation	Reference initials
Body of the letter	

This section will discuss these various parts in detail. Before reading further, however, locate each of these parts on the diagram so that you will be familiar with their position.

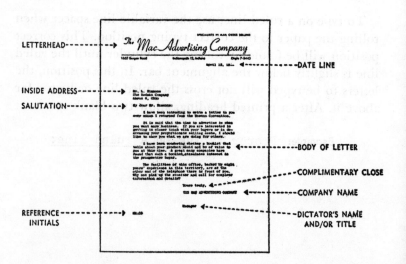

In addition to the more common parts shown on the previous page, some letters may also include:

Attention line   Carbon copy notation
Subject or "re" line   Postscript
Enclosure notation

The position of these additional parts will also be discussed in the following pages.

When studying the various parts of a business letter in the pages that follow, pay particular attention to the vertical spacing—the number of blank lines to be left above and below each part. **Except for the space above the inside address, these never vary.** Later in this section, when studying punctuation and letter styles, you will learn the proper punctuation to use, and the correct horizontal placement.

LETTERHEAD

The letterhead is the stationery used by a company for its correspondence. The printed material at the top of the page usually contains the firm name, address, and telephone number. It may also contain a company slogan and the names of the officers of the firm. This printed material normally occupies approximately two inches at the top of the page (12 typewriter lines).

DATE LINE

The horizontal placement of the date line—whether flush left, centered, or flush right—depends upon the letter style used. The variation of its position on the line will be explained as each letter style is shown in the following pages. In every letter style, however, the following rules will apply to the typing of the date line:

1. Type the date line two lines below the printed letter-head—usually on the fourteenth line.
2. Spell the name of the month in full.
3. Do not use *d, nd, st, th,* or *rd* after the day of the month.
4. The day of the month is separated from the year by a comma.

April 18, 19--   May 1, 19--   June 3, 19--

INSIDE ADDRESS

The inside address indicates the person—or organization—to whom the letter is directed.

Its placement on the page—the number of blank lines to be left between the top of the page and the inside address—depends upon the length of the letter. (This is discussed in detail on page 238.)

The inside address usually contains the following information:

Name and/or Title of the Addressee

1. If both the name and title are used, separate them by a comma when typed on a single line.
2. If the name and title are so long as to unbalance the other lines, the title should be typed alone on a second line. Note that no comma is needed in this case.

Mr. C. Brown, President   Mr. C. Brown
                               Assistant Director

Name of Company

1. Type the company's name exactly as it appears on the firm's letterhead. Do not substitute *and* for & and do not omit the word *The* if it is included in the letterhead.
2. If the name of the company requires an additional line, indent the second line five spaces.

```
Mr. C. Brown, President
The Acme Corporation


Mr. C. Brown, President
The American Distribution
     & Supply Corporation
```

Building Number and Street Name

1. Use figures for all building numbers except *One*.

```
One Forest Road          6 Forest Road
```

2. Use figures for street (avenue, etc.) names above *Ten*. Omit *d, st, nd, rd,* and *th* after street or avenue numbers.

```
Second Avenue            12 Avenue
```

3. Use a dash to separate building numbers from street *numbers*.

```
6740 — 45 Street      6740 Grove Street
```

4. Spell out directions such as *North, South, East,* and *West,* but sections of the city such as *Northwest,* or *Southeast* should be abbreviated. In typing these abbreviations, space once after the periods.

```
12 North Grove Street    27 Ninth Avenue S. E.
```

City, Zone, and State

1. Type the city and state on one line with a comma separating them.

2. If a zone number is used, a comma is placed only between the zone number and the state.

   ```
   Akron 14, Ohio
   ```

3. Do not abbreviate the name of a state, with the exception of *D. C.* for the *District of Columbia* and *N. Y.* when it follows *New York*.

   ```
   Mr. C. Brown, President
   The Acme Corporation
   One East 45 Street
   Seattle 3, Washington
   ```

   ```
   Mr. C. Brown, President
   The Acme Corporation
   852 G Street N. W.
   Washington 7, D. C.
   ```

   ```
   Mr. C. Brown, President
   The Acme Corporation
   32 North 24 Street
   New York 37, N. Y.
   ```

4. If an address requires only two lines, it is preferable to expand it to three lines by typing the state on a line by itself.

   ```
   Miss Anna Lee Porter
   Sweetwater
   Texas
   ```

ATTENTION LINE

The attention line is used to expedite the delivery of the letter to the proper individual or department.

1. The attention line is typed between the inside address and the salutation, with one blank line above and below it. It is either flush left, or centered on the line, and may be underscored.

2. Whenever the attention line is used, the salutation must be *Gentlemen:* (See sample on page 251.)

```
Martin Enterprises, Inc.
406 East Fourth Street
Cleveland 13, Ohio
x
Attention:  Mr. James Foster
x
Gentlemen:
```

> Hereafter, the mark x is used to indicate each blank line.

SALUTATION

When a letter is addressed to an individual, the salutation should be directed to that individual. If no name is indicated, you may use any appropriate salutation.

1. Type the salutation at the left margin, two lines below the last line of the inside address or attention line.

2. Names and titles are always capitalized, but adjectives are not capitalized unless they begin the salutation.

```
Dear Sir:              Dear Mr. Foster:
My dear Sir:           My dear Dr. Jones:
```

SUBJECT OR "RE" LINE

The purpose of the subject or "re" line is to give the reader a preview of the contents to be found in the letter without his having to read it through completely. Type the subject line two lines below the salutation, either flush left or centered on the line. (Some firms prefer to have the subject line typed two lines *above* the salutation.) See sample on page 250.

```
Gentlemen:
x
Subject:  Television Advertising
x
You will be glad to know that Channel 3
```

A subject line that requires more than one line may be typed as follows:

```
Subject:  Television Advertising
          Rates as of June 9
```

THE BODY

The message that the letter contains is called the body of the letter. The form in which the body is typed will depend upon the style that is used, but *in all cases,* you must *double space* between paragraphs.

When the body is double spaced, the first line of each paragraph must be indented five spaces or multiples of five. This is best accomplished by setting a tabulator stop rather than using the space bar. In addition, set the line space regulator for double spacing. Thus you need only throw the carriage return lever once at the end of each line. Note that in both single-spaced and double-spaced letters there is only one blank line between paragraphs. Note also that in a double-spaced letter only the body of the letter is double-spaced; the other elements remain unchanged. (See sample on page 252.)

If a letter contains numbered paragraphs, double space both before and after the numbered material to separate it from the body of the letter, and also double space between each numbered paragraph. In addition, the left margin is indented five spaces, while the right margin remains unchanged. Note the example on page 250.

If the body of a letter contains quoted material, the same double spacing is used as applied to numbered paragraphs—double spacing before, between, and after each paragraph. However, the quoted paragraph is indented five spaces from *each* margin.

One of our dealers wrote to us just the other day:

> "Your national advertising campaign has enabled us to double our sales in the past month."

You will be happy to know that we are planning to repeat this campaign next month.

COMPLIMENTARY CLOSE

The complimentary close should express the feeling that the dictator or writer wishes to convey. For example, if the salutation is informal, the complimentary close should also be informal.

1. Type the complimentary close two lines below the last line of the body of the letter. (Examples on next page.)
2. Capitalize only the first word of a complimentary close.

COMPANY NAME

1. The company name is typed two lines below the complimentary close. (Examples on next page.)
2. It is always typed in capital letters.
3. The company name may be omitted, particularly when using an informal complimentary close, such as *Sincerely.*

DICTATOR'S NAME AND/OR TITLE

1. The dictator's name and/or title is typed four lines below the company name. This allows three blank lines for the signature.
2. The dictator's title may follow his name, with a comma separating them; or the title may be typed directly beneath the name, in which case no punctuation is used after the name.
3. The dictator's name may be omitted and just the title used.
4. Note the use of a woman's name in the closing. The notation *Miss* or *Mrs.* is typed, in parentheses, before the name.

```
x                              x
Very truly yours,              Sincerely,
x                              x
MARTIN ENTERPRISES             x
x                              x
x                              James Foster
x                              Director
James Foster, Director


x                              x
Very truly yours,              Very truly yours,
x                              x
MARTIN ENTERPRISES             MARTIN ENTERPRISES
x                              x
x                              x
x                              x
Director                       (Miss) Janet Berney
                               Secretary to Mr. Foster
```

REFERENCE INITIALS

The reference initials contain the initials of the dictator and the secretary.

1. They are typed flush with the left margin.
2. They may be typed on the same line as the dictator's name or one or two lines below it.
3. The dictator's initials are typed first, followed by the secretary's. They are separated from each other by a diagonal (/) or a colon (:). There are many acceptable forms:

HJ:rc   J:c   HJ:RC   HJ/RC

HJones/rc   HJ/rc

ENCLOSURE NOTATION

To assist the secretary and the person who receives the letter, it is customary to indicate the inclusion of any pieces of literature or other matter with the letter. This notice is the enclosure notation. (See sample on page 259.)

1. The enclosure notation is typed flush with the left margin. It may be typed one or two lines below the reference initials.
2. If there is one enclosure, the word *Enclosure,* or *Enc.,* should be used. If there is more than one enclosure, the number of enclosures should follow the reference. Some firms prefer listing each enclosure.

Enc.   Enclosure

Enc. (3)   Enclosures 2

Enclosures: Return Envelope
              Catalog

COPY NOTATION

A letter addressed to one person may be of importance to another individual or group of individuals and copies of the original letter may be sent to these interested parties. In such cases, a notation is made at the bottom of the letter to indicate to the addressee that these copies have been forwarded.

1. Type the copy notation flush with the left margin, two spaces below the reference initials or enclosure notation.
2. Special paper, usually onion skin, is generally used for copy sheets. In such cases, the word "COPY" is printed on the copy sheet.
3. The copy notation on the original letter may be indicated as follows:

```
cc Mr. James Gordon

Copy to The Empire Press, Inc.

c.c. to Mr. A. M. Richards
        Mr. William Young
```

POSTSCRIPT

A postscript is an afterthought that is added to the letter after it has been dictated or typed. It is rarely used in business letters, but every secretary should be familiar with it.

1. The abbreviation *P. S.* is used to identify the postscript.
2. The postscript is typed two lines below the reference initials or below the last notation in the letter.
3. It is typed flush with the left margin, but if indented paragraphs are used in the letter, the postscript may also be indented.

```
RES:SL
x
Enc.
x
P. S. Your order was sent on April 18.
```

PUNCTUATION

There are three forms of punctuation that may be employed in typing a business letter:

1. Mixed—Most common form used.
2. Close—Occasionally used.
3. Open—Infrequently used.

Although any one of the three is considered correct in the business world, the mixed form is used most frequently. The decision as to which form to use, however, will depend upon the office in which you are employed.

MIXED PUNCTUATION

1. No marks of punctuation are used after the date or after any of the lines of the inside address.
2. A colon is typed after the salutation.
3. A comma is typed after the complimentary close line.

```
January 5, 19--


Armour Enterprises
1273 Forest Road
Birmingham 7, Alabama

Dear Mr. Barnes:


Very truly yours,

BENSON & SON, INC.



Arthur Benson, President
```

CLOSE PUNCTUATION

1. A period is typed after the date, attention, and "re" lines.
2. A comma is typed at the end of each line in the inside address except the last, which is ended with a period.
3. A colon is typed after the salutation.
4. A comma is typed after the complimentary close and the firm name, and a period is typed after the dictator's name or title.

```
              January 5, 19--.


         Armour Enterprises,
         1273 Forest Road,
         Birmingham 7, Alabama.

         Dear Mr. Barnes:



         Very truly yours,

         BENSON & SON, INC.,



         Arthur Benson, President.
```

OPEN PUNCTUATION

1. All marks of punctuation are omitted after the date and after all lines in the inside address.
2. The colon is omitted after the salutation.
3. All marks of punctuation are omitted after all lines in the closing. However, if a line ends with an abbreviation, such as *Inc.,* the period must be shown.

January 5, 19--

Armour Enterprises
1273 Forest Road
Birmingham 7, Alabama

Dear Mr. Barnes

Very truly yours

BENSON & SON, INC.

Arthur Benson, President

LETTER PLACEMENT

The placement of a letter on a page depends upon the length of the letter. For proper balance, both the margins and the position of the inside address must be varied for letters of different lengths. Eventually, a glance at your notes will enable you to judge the placement of your letter, but this requires a good deal of practice and experience. For the present, make use of the procedure given below as a guide to proper placement.

First: Determine the number of words in the body of the letter to be typed. To do this:

1. Count the number of words on any three lines of your shorthand notes.
2. Divide this number by three to obtain the average number of words on each line.
3. Multiply this average by the number of lines of shorthand notes in the body of the letter. Your answer represents the approximate number of words in the body of the letter.

Then refer to the following chart:

CLASSIFICATION	WORDS IN BODY OF THE LETTER	MARGINS		LINES TO IN-SIDE ADDRESS
		PICA	ELITE	
SHORT	TO 50	18-68	26-76	24
	75	18-68	26-76	23
	100	18-68	21-81	22
AVERAGE	125	18-68	21-81	21
	150	18-68	21-81	20
	175	18-68	21-81	19
	200	18-68	21-81	18
LONG	225	12-72	16-86	20
	250	12-72	16-86	19
	275	12-72	16-86	18
TWO-PAGE	300+	12-72	16-86	18

NOTES ON THE USE OF THE CHART

The chart on the facing page is for 8½ x 11-inch paper, and is only a *guide* to letter placement. It should not be considered a rigid, inflexible rule that must be followed without variations. Letters that contain special features, such as a great deal of indented material, will make adjustments in the chart necessary, and the secretary must therefore use the chart with good judgment and understanding.

Date Line:	Two lines below letterhead, except in the personal style which is explained below.
Double-spaced Letters:	To determine the correct placement for a double-spaced letter, multiply the number of words in the body of the letter by two and then refer to the chart. The inside address is single spaced except in the indented style, where it may be double spaced. Also see page 230.
Personal Style Letters:	Plain paper is used for personal letters and the date line is typed 14 lines from the top of the page. If the sender's address is to be typed above the date, the address will start on the twelfth line. Also see pages 264, 265 and the sample letter on page 270.
Tabulation in a Letter:	If a letter contains tabulated material, see pages 184 and 198.

LETTER STYLES

There are many different letter styles in use today and a good secretary should be familiar with the most common styles.

During your course you will transcribe letters in various styles, but when you obtain your first position as a secretary, you should study the style used by your employer and use it in all future letters.

Letter styles can be grouped into two basic forms:

BLOCK FORM
INDENTED FORM

All other letter styles are merely variations of these two basic forms.

In business today you will most often see the four styles shown below and on the facing page.

FULL BLOCK STYLE   STANDARD BLOCK STYLE

At first glance there may seem to be many details to be learned. Actually this is not the case. Study the examples for a moment. Notice that in each of the styles the space between parts of the letter remains unchanged—only the position of each line from left to right changes.

Since you will often wish to move the carriage to a specific point—five spaces in for paragraph indentations or the center of the page for the complimentary close—review the use of the tabulating mechanism.

On the following pages, these four styles are explained in detail. To further clarify the examples, the mark "x" is used to indicate each blank line. (Remember, to leave *one* blank line you must throw the carriage return lever *two* times—always once more than the number of blank lines required.)

When studying samples of each of these styles, note in particular the placement of attention line, subject or "re" line, and the enclosure and carbon copy notations.

| SEMIBLOCK STYLE | INDENTED STYLE |

STANDARD BLOCK STYLE LETTER

Date Line: Centered or ending flush right.

Inside Address: Flush with left margin.

Attention Line: Flush with left margin, or centered, two lines below inside address.

Salutation: Flush with left margin, two lines below inside address or *attention* line.

Subject or "Re" Line: Flush with left margin, or centered, two lines below salutation. Must conform in placement with *attention* line if both are used. (Not shown in sample—see page 250.)

Body: All paragraphs flush with left margin. Start two lines below *subject* or *re* line or salutation. Single space, except between paragraphs.

Complimentary Close: Start at center point of page, two lines below body.

Firm Name: In capital letters, start at center point of page, two lines below complimentary close.

Dictator's Name and/or Title: Start at center point of page, four lines below firm name.

Reference Initials: Flush with left margin.

Enclosure Notation: Flush with left margin, two lines below reference initials.

The Mac Advertising Company

1350 Bergen Road   Indianapolis 12, Indiana   EAgle 7-3440

x
January 14, 19 - -

Johnson Fabrics, Inc.
East Compton Road
Youngstown 27, Ohio
x
Attention: Mr. Roger Johnson
x
Gentlemen:
x

x
Very truly yours,
x
THE MAC ADVERTISING CO.
x
x
x
Edward R. Jones
Director

x
ERJ:ch
x
Enclosure

STANDARD BLOCK STYLE
Also see pages 250, 258 and 259.

SEMIBLOCK STYLE LETTER

The semiblock style is set up the same as the standard block style, with these exceptions:

Attention Line: Centered, two lines below inside address. (Not shown in sample—see example on page 251.)

Subject or "Re" Line: Centered, two lines below salutation.

Body: All paragraphs are indented. Most firms prefer a five-space indentation, although multiples of five are permissible. Set a tabulator stop instead of striking the space bar repeatedly.

May be single spaced or double spaced. (See sample on page 252.)

The Mac Advertising Company

1350 Bergen Road   Indianapolis 12, Indiana   EAgle 7-3440

x
January 14, 19 - -

Johnson Fabrics, Inc.
East Compton Road
Youngstown 27, Ohio
x
Gentlemen:
x
         Subject: Fabric 370
x

‖‖‖
‖‖‖
‖‖‖
‖‖‖
‖‖‖

‖‖‖
‖‖‖
‖‖‖
‖‖‖
‖‖‖

‖‖‖
‖‖‖
‖‖‖
‖‖‖
‖‖‖
‖‖‖‖‖‖‖‖‖‖‖‖‖‖‖‖‖‖‖‖‖‖‖‖‖‖‖‖‖‖‖‖‖‖‖‖‖‖‖

         x
         Very truly yours,
         x
         THE MAC ADVERTISING CO.
         x
         x
         x
         Edward R. Jones, Director

x
ERJ:ch

SEMIBLOCK STYLE
Also see pages 251, 252 and 270.

FULL BLOCK STYLE LETTER

The full block style is a newcomer to the business world. It is becoming more and more popular, however, with the large business firms. Actually it is very much like the standard block style—the only differences occurring in the date line and the closing.

The reason for the growing popularity of this form lies in the ease of typing the letter. Everything is flush with the left margin. This eliminates the necessity of centering or using the tabular stops—a time saver.

Date Line: Flush with left margin.

Complimentary Close: Flush with left margin.

Firm Name: Flush with left margin. Note that the firm name may be omitted from any style letter, as it has in this example.

Dictator's Name and/or Title: Flush with left margin, four lines below firm name or complimentary close.

Postscript: Two lines below reference initials. Usually typed flush with left margin. (In semiblock or indented styles the *P.S.* may be indented as many spaces as the paragraphs in the body of the letter.)

The Mac Advertising Company

1350 Bergen Road   Indianapolis 12, Indiana   EAgle 7-3440

x
January 14, 19- -

Mr. Roger Johnson
Johnson Fabrics, Inc.
East Compton Road
Youngstown 27, Ohio
x
Dear Mr. Johnson:
x
Re: Account 3705
x

x
Very truly yours,
x
x
x
Edward R. Jones, Director
x
ERJ:ch
x
P. S.																																																																	

FULL BLOCK STYLE
Also see page 253.

INDENTED STYLE LETTER

The indented style is similar to the semiblock style, except for the inside address and closing.

Date Line: Centered or ending flush right.

Inside Address: The first line of the inside address is flush with the left margin. The second line is indented five spaces from the left margin. The third line is indented five spaces further than the second line. Additional lines would each be indented five spaces from the one above it.

Attention Line: Centered, two lines below the inside address. (Not shown in sample.)

Subject or "Re" Line: Centered, two lines below the salutation. (Not shown in sample.)

Body: All paragraphs are indented the same as in the semiblock style—five spaces or multiples of five. May be single spaced or double spaced.

Complimentary Close: Start at center point of page, two lines below body.

Firm Name: In capital letters, indented five spaces from the complimentary close and two lines below it.

Dictator's Name and/or Title: Indent five spaces from the firm name and four lines below it.

Copy Notation: Either flush left or indented.

The Mac Advertising Company

1350 Bergen Road   Indianapolis 12, Indiana   EAgle 7-3440

x
January 14, 19 – – .

Johnson Fabrics, Inc.
   East Compton Road
     Youngstown 27, Ohio

x
Dear Mr. Johnson:
x

    ||||||||||||||||||||||||||||||||||||||||||||||||||||||||||||||||||||

    ||||||||||||||||||||||||||||||||||||||||||||||||||||||||||||||||||||

    ||||||||||||||||||||||||||||||||||||||||||||||||||||||||||||||||||||

               x
               Very truly yours,
               x
               THE MAC ADVERTISING CO.
                  x
                  x
                  x
                 E. R. Jones, Director

x
ERJ:ch
x
Copy to Mr. E. R. Brown

INDENTED STYLE LETTER

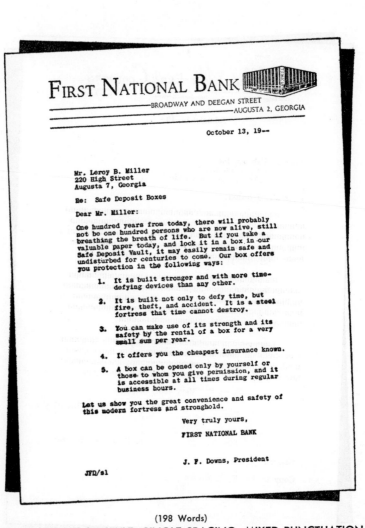

(198 Words)

STANDARD BLOCK STYLE—SINGLE SPACING—MIXED PUNCTUATION

Note numbered paragraphs in the body of the letter and the location of "re" line.

Barrett Furniture Company

4709 East 13th Avenue
Detroit 17, Michigan
GReenview 6-1080

May 12, 19--.

Martin Manufacturing Company,
15 South Wabash Avenue,
Chicago 14, Illinois.

        Attention· Mr. George H. Reynolds

Gentlemen:

        Does your filing system ever go on strike? Does it ever refuse to give up instantly the information that you know it holds?

        Unless all your filing devices minimize the moves necessary in the transaction and recording of business, they make you the victim and not the master of details. Your valuable papers and records must not only be safe, but must be available to facilitate and accelerate the dispatch of business.

        Our cabinets are built for use. You select and arrange a cabinet to suit your requirements, and don't have to adjust your requirements to suit the cabinet.

        Why not call us for complete information?

              Yours very truly,

              BARRETT FURNITURE COMPANY,

              J. C. Barrett President

JCB:AR

(105 Words)

SEMIBLOCK STYLE—SINGLE SPACING—CLOSE PUNCTUATION

Note position of attention line. It may be centered, as above, or may start flush left, depending upon the letter style. (See page 229.)

252

PORTER CABLE
BLACK AND DECKER
STANLEY-DEWALT
HOUSEHOLD APPLIANCES

BLAKELY HARDWARE COMPANY

Starr & Borden Avenues
Albany 14, New York
ROosevelt 4-2200
PAINTS — WALLPAPER

October 23, 19--

Mrs. George Armstrong
29 State Street
Albany 7, New York

Dear Mrs. Armstrong:

We are sorry to learn that the wrong merchandise was delivered to you in our shipment of October 12.

The wall and woodwork cleaner that should have been delivered is being put on our truck this afternoon, and you will no doubt receive it before the end of the week. We have also made arrangements for our driver to pick up the four cans of plastic varnish that were delivered in error.

We hope to have the opportunity to serve you in a much more satisfactory manner in the very near future

Very truly yours,

BLAKELY HARDWARE COMPANY

M. H. Lynn
Secretary to Mr. Blakely

MHL

(93 Words)
SEMIBLOCK STYLE—DOUBLE SPACING—MIXED PUNCTUATION
Note reference initials used when typist composes the letter herself.

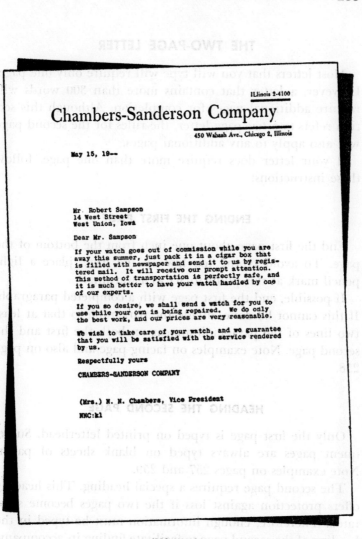

ILlinois 2-4100

Chambers-Sanderson Company

450 Wabash Ave., Chicago 2, Illinois

May 15, 19--

Mr. Robert Sampson
14 West Street
West Union, Iowa

Dear Mr. Sampson

If your watch goes out of commission while you are
away this summer, just pack it in a cigar box that
is filled with newspaper and send it to us by registered mail. It will receive our prompt attention.
This method of transportation is perfectly safe, and
it is much better to have your watch handled by one
of our experts.

If you so desire, we shall send a watch for you to
use while your own is being repaired. We do only
the best work, and our prices are very reasonable.

We wish to take care of your watch, and we guarantee
that you will be satisfied with the service rendered
by us.

Respectfully yours

CHAMBERS-SANDERSON COMPANY

(Mrs.) N. N. Chambers, Vice President
NNC:kl

(113 Words)
FULL BLOCK STYLE—SINGLE SPACING—OPEN PUNCTUATION
Note woman's signature in closing.

THE TWO-PAGE LETTER

Most letters that you will type will require only one page. However, a letter that contains more than 300 words will require additional pages for completion. Although this section refers to a *two*-page letter, the rules for the second page will also apply to any additional pages.

If your letter does require more than one page, follow these instructions:

ENDING THE FIRST PAGE

End the first page about one inch from the bottom of the page. To avoid typing too low on the page, place a light pencil mark at this point to act as a warning.

If possible, end the first page with a completed paragraph. If this cannot be done, divide the paragraph so that at least two lines of the paragraph appear on both the first and the second page. Note examples on facing page and also on page 258.

HEADING THE SECOND PAGE

Only the first page is typed on printed letterhead. Subsequent pages are always typed on blank sheets of paper. Note examples on pages 257 and 259.

The second page requires a special heading. This heading offers protection against loss if the two pages become separated. Therefore, enough information must be typed in the heading of the second page to facilitate finding its accompanying sheet.

This heading is typed six to nine spaces from the top of the page, and must include the following information:

FILE NAME　　　　　PAGE NUMBER　　　　　DATE

The Mac Advertising Company

1300 Bergen Road   Indianapolis 12, Indiana   EAgle 7-3440

January 14, 19 - -

Mr. Roger Johnson, Director
Johnson Fabrics, Inc.
East Compton Road
Youngstown 27, Ohio

Dear Mr. Johnson:

TWO-PAGE LETTER
Continued on page 257

The FILE NAME will depend upon the filing system employed by your firm. In most cases, the file name will be the name of the firm to whom you are writing and not the name of the individual addressed.

The PAGE NUMBER is typed on the same line as the file name, and is centered on the page if possible, or centered in the space left between the file name and the date. In either of these cases, type the number alone or type the number with a hyphen before and after it. However, in the full block style, it is correct to use the phrase "Page 2." (See example at bottom of page.)

The DATE is typed so that it ends flush with the right margin.

Here is a typical second-page heading:

Johnson Brothers, Inc.　　　　　　-2-　　　　　　May 14, 19—

If a great deal of correspondence is carried on with more than one individual of a firm, type his name flush left, directly above the file name.

In some cases, where the central office has many branches, it is necessary to identify the branch. This is shown in the full block sample, below.

If the full block style is used, the second page is headed as follows:

Johnson Brothers, Inc., N Y. C.
Page 2
May 14, 19—

After typing the proper heading allow two or three blank lines before continuing the letter.

Johnson Fabrics, Inc.   - 2 -   January 14, 19 - -

‖‖
‖‖
‖‖
‖‖
‖‖‖

‖‖‖
‖‖
‖‖
‖‖
‖‖‖

‖‖‖
‖‖‖

Very truly yours,

THE MAC ADVERTISING CO.

Edward R. Jones
Director

ERJ:ch

Copy to Mr. E. R. Brown

TWO-PAGE LETTER
Also see pages 258 and 259.

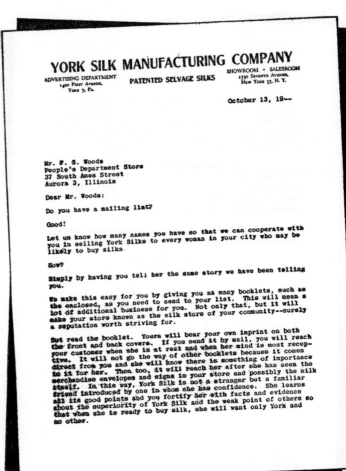

YORK SILK MANUFACTURING COMPANY

ADVERTISING DEPARTMENT
1400 First Avenue,
York 7, Pa.

PATENTED SELVAGE SILKS

SHOWROOM · SALESROOM
1730 Seventh Avenue,
New York 37, N. Y.

October 13, 19--

Mr. F. S. Woods
People's Department Store
37 South Ames Street
Aurora 3, Illinois

Dear Mr. Woods:

Do you have a mailing list?

Good!

Let us know how many names you have so that we can cooperate with you in selling York Silks to every woman in your city who may be likely to buy silks.

How?

Simply by having you tell her the same story we have been telling you.

We make this easy for you by giving you as many booklets, such as the enclosed, as you need to send to your list. This will mean a lot of additional business for you. Not only that, but it will make your store known as the silk store of your community--surely a reputation worth striving for.

But read the booklet. Yours will bear your own imprint on both the front and back covers. If you send it by mail, you will reach your customer when she is at rest and when her mind is most receptive. It will not go the way of other booklets because it comes direct from you and she will know there is something of importance in it for her. Then too, it will reach her after she has seen the merchandise envelopes and signs in your store and possibly the silk itself. In this way, York Silk is not a stranger but a familiar friend introduced by one in whom she has confidence. She learns all its good points and you fortify her with facts and evidence about the superiority of York Silk and the weak point of others so that when she is ready to buy silk, she will want only York and no other.

TWO-PAGE LETTER—SEE FACING PAGE

People's Department Store   -2-   October 13, 19---

The merchandise envelopes, booklets, signs, electrotypes or mats of advertisements, and other selling helps will be forwarded as soon as we hear from you.

If we can be of help to you, or if there is any information you require, please do not hesitate to write to us.

                       Yours truly,

                       YORK SILK MANUFACTURING COMPANY

                       (Miss) Mary Ruth Brown
                       Advertising Manager

MRB:PL

Enc

(325 Words)

TWO-PAGE LETTER—STANDARD BLOCK STYLE—SINGLE SPACING—MIXED PUNCTUATION

Note heading for the second page. (See pages 254-259.)

OVERHANGING STYLE

This style, though rarely employed, is generally used in advertising letters. It is identical to the standard block style except for the body of the letter:

Body: The first line of each paragraph starts at the left margin and all other lines are indented five spaces or multiples of five.

The **Mac** *Advertising* **Company**

1350 Bergen Road   Indianapolis 12, Indiana   EAgle 7-3440

x
January 14, 19 - -

Johnson Fabrics, Inc.
East Compton Road
Youngstown 27, Ohio
x
Attention: Mr. Roger Johnson
x
Gentlemen:
x

x
Very truly yours,
x
THE MAC ADVERTISING CO.
x
x
x
Edward R. Jones
Director

x
ERJ:ch
x
Enclosure

OVERHANGING STYLE

NOMA STYLE

This style was introduced many years ago by the National Office Management Association in an attempt to provide a simplified letter style.

It is similar to the full block style in that everything is typed flush left. However, the salutation, complimentary close, and company name are all omitted. In addition, note the following special features:

Subject or "Re" Line: Must be included. The word "Subject" or "Re" is not typed, but the subject of the letter is typed all in capital letters, *three* lines below the inside address.

Dictator's Name and/or Title: Typed all in capital letters, *four* lines below body.

Reference Initials: The typist's initials *only* are typed two lines below dictator's name and/or title.

The *Mac Advertising Company*

1330 Bergen Road   Indianapolis 12, Indiana   EAgle 7-3440

January 14, 19 - -

Johnson Fabrics, Inc.
East Compton Road
Youngstown 27, Ohio

ADVERTISING

EDWARD R. JONES, DIRECTOR

ch

NOMA STYLE

PERSONAL AND INFORMAL LETTERS

The letter styles you have just studied are those that are used for correspondence in the business world. However, when writing informal business letters or personal letters, a less formal style is used.

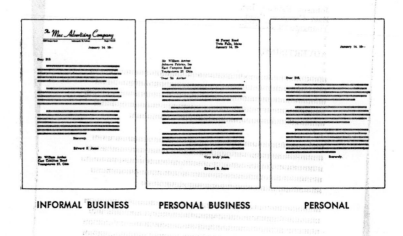

INFORMAL BUSINESS   PERSONAL BUSINESS   PERSONAL

INFORMAL BUSINESS LETTERS

Social or personal business letters can be typed in any of the styles previously explained, or can be set up in the informal business letter style. In this style, the inside address is "dropped" below the closing and is typed at the left-hand margin, two lines below the dictator's name. Because of its informal nature, no title or reference initials are used in the closing.

In planning the placement of this style, refer to the chart on page 238 and type the salutation on the line indicated for the first line of the inside address.

PERSONAL BUSINESS LETTERS

Formal or business letters that you, as an individual, write, such as an application for a position or a letter of inquiry to a company, should be typed on plain white paper in the personal business style. Basically, this style is set up the same as a regular business letter but the sender's address is included above the date line, and the reference initials are omitted. See the example on page 270.

PERSONAL LETTERS

Letters that you write to friends and acquaintances are typed on plain white paper. This style does not include the normal parts of a business letter and requires only the date, salutation, and complimentary close. The salutation is followed by a comma instead of a colon.

For proper placement of either of the personal-style letters, follow the chart on page 238 and note in particular the special instructions facing the chart pertaining to personal letters.

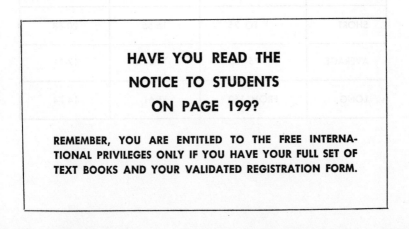

HAVE YOU READ THE
NOTICE TO STUDENTS
ON PAGE 199?

REMEMBER, YOU ARE ENTITLED TO THE FREE INTERNATIONAL PRIVILEGES ONLY IF YOU HAVE YOUR FULL SET OF TEXT BOOKS AND YOUR VALIDATED REGISTRATION FORM.

SMALL LETTERHEADS

Although most business correspondence is typed on stationery that is 8½ x 11 inches in size, there are some companies that use a smaller size for notes and short letters. Most common among these are the "Executive" which measures 7¼ x 10½ inches, and the half-size letterhead that is only 5½ x 8½ inches in size.

EXECUTIVE SIZE

When typing letters on executive-size stationery, determine the position for the inside address by referring to the chart on page 238 and use the following chart as a general guide to margin settings:

LENGTH	WORDS IN BODY OF THE LETTER	MARGINS	
		PICA	ELITE
SHORT	TO 75	16-56	20-68
AVERAGE	75-150	14-59	17-71
LONG	FROM 150	11-61	14-74

HALF SIZE

When typing letters on half-size letterhead, first adjust the paper bail rollers. Then follow these instructions:

Style:
If the letter to be typed is extremely short, it is usually advisable to use double spacing for the body of the letter. This, of course, means that each paragraph will start with a five-space indentation. If single spacing is used, however, the letter may be typed in any of the accepted styles.

Margins:
Allow three-quarters to one inch for each margin.

Date Line:
Two lines below the printed letterhead.

Inside Address:
Four to six lines below the date, depending upon the length of the letter.

Closing:
Starts at the center of the page—Pica, 27; Elite, 33.

ENVELOPES

The most common envelope in business use today measures 9½ x 4⅛ inches and is referred to as a "No. 10" envelope. Of the smaller envelopes, the No. 6¾ is the most popular, measuring 6½ x 3⅝ inches.

THE RETURN ADDRESS

The return address is generally printed in the upper left corner. If it is not, type it single spaced, one-half inch from the left edge, starting on the third line.

THE ADDRESS

The address on an envelope should conform in both style and punctuation to that used in the inside address. Thus, if the inside address is indented, the address on the envelope should be indented. The only exception to this is that a three-line address—whether indented or blocked—may be double spaced, and an address that requires four or more lines should be single spaced.

The rules governing the typing of the address on the envelope are the same as those given for the inside address on pages 226-228. However, the state may be typed all in capital letters.

When using a No. 10 envelope, type the address 14 lines down from the top of the envelope, starting approximately 5 spaces to the left of the center of the envelope. When using smaller envelopes, type the address 12 spaces down, starting —as before—approximately 5 spaces to the left of center.

SPECIAL NOTATIONS

The type of service that a letter is to receive, such as **Air Mail**, Special Delivery, Registered, etc., is typed below **the** area allowed for the stamp. It may be typed all in **capital** letters.

Other notations, such as Personal, Attention, Please Forward, etc., are typed two lines below the last line of the address, starting one-half inch from the left edge of the envelope. The notation may be underscored, typed all in capital letters, or both. A one-word notation, if typed all in capital letters, can be "expanded" by spacing once after each letter.

BARRETT FURNITURE COMPANY
4709 East 16th Avenue
Detroit 17, Michigan

AIR MAIL

Roger Paper Company
1347 Village Avenue
Phoenix 17, Arizona

Attention: Mr. H. Porter

BARRETT FURNITURE COMPANY
4709 East 16th Avenue
Detroit 17, Michigan

Roger Paper Company,

1347 Village Avenue,

Phoenix 17, ARIZONA

BARRETT FURNITURE COMPANY
4709 East 16th Avenue
Detroit 17, Michigan

Mr. Harold Porter, Manager
Roger Paper Company
1347 Village Avenue
Phoenix 17, ARIZONA

P E R S O N A L

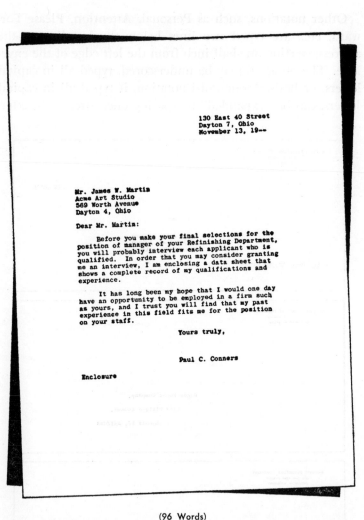

130 East 40 Street
Dayton 7, Ohio
November 13, 19--

Mr. James W. Martin
Acme Art Studio
569 Worth Avenue
Dayton 4, Ohio

Dear Mr. Martin:

Before you make your final selections for the
position of manager of your Refinishing Department,
you will probably interview each applicant who is
qualified. In order that you may consider granting
me an interview, I am enclosing a data sheet that
shows a complete record of my qualifications and
experience.

It has long been my hope that I would one day
have an opportunity to be employed in a firm such
as yours, and I trust you will find that my past
experience in this field fits me for the position
on your staff.

Yours truly,

Paul C. Conners

Enclosure

(96 Words)

PERSONAL BUSINESS LETTER—SEMIBLOCK STYLE—SINGLE SPACING— MIXED PUNCTUATION

Note position of return address. (See page 265.)

SUBMITTING THE LETTER FOR SIGNATURE

Before taking your letter out of the machine, check it carefully for any errors that you may have overlooked. Then assemble your letter and carbon copies in the following order:

1. The envelope, with the original copy inserted under its flap, is placed on top.

2. Under this, all carbon copies, properly designated for forwarding to other departments or individuals.

3. The file copy, attached to the original correspondence, is at the bottom of the pile.

FOLDING AND INSERTING THE LETTER

Before folding your letter for insertion into an envelope, make a final check to be sure that the letter is signed, that all corrections have been made, that all enclosures have been included, and that you have the *correct* envelope. Then:

1. Place letter on the desk, face up.

2. Fold up the bottom third of the paper, being careful to line up the edges of the paper before making the crease.

3. Fold down upper part of paper to bring the top edge to the first crease.

4. Insert any enclosures *within* the folded letter.

5. Insert letter with the single edge first, as shown.

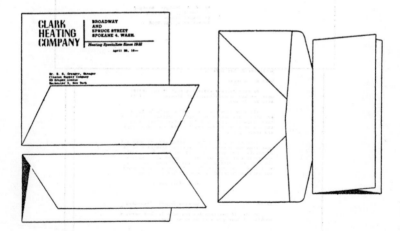

MAILING THE LETTER

Once you have inserted the letter and sealed the envelope—making certain that the letter is in the correct envelope and that any inserts have been enclosed—you have to choose the type of postal service the letter is to receive.

The following paragraphs will give you both the general information about each class of service and the rates in effect as this book went to press. However, since postal rates are constantly changing, it is best to contact your post office to verify these rates.

Since the amount of postage is determined by the weight of the mailing, it is best to have an accurate postal scale on hand so that you do not waste stamps by applying too much postage, or annoy your customers with postage-due mail.

FIRST-CLASS MAIL

First-class mail includes any typewritten or handwritten matter (including carbon copies), private mailing cards or postal cards, and any matter sealed against inspection. Thus, all your typewritten letters must be sent by first-class mail.

RATES

In the following rates a single asterisk (*) means that the rate applies for the weight shown or any fraction thereof.

A double asterisk (**) indicates that the rates shown are *in addition to* the regular rate.

FIRST-CLASS MAIL

Letters ......3¢ per oz.*
Government Postal
    Cards ....2¢ each

AIR MAIL

Air mail is the fastest means of having your letter delivered to a *distant* city.

In order to make certain that the post office recognizes that air-mail service is wanted, it is best to use the special red, white, and blue envelopes available for this purpose. Otherwise you can use air-mail stamps alone, or regular stamps if you type A I R   M A I L below the stamps.

AIR MAIL

Letters ......6¢ per oz.*
Post Cards ......4¢ each

SECOND-CLASS MAIL

Second-class matter includes magazines, newspapers, and similar periodicals and is handled at a special low rate.

SECOND-CLASS MAIL

2¢ for first 2 oz.
1¢ for each additional 2 oz.*

THIRD-CLASS MAIL

Third-class matter includes books, catalogs, printed circulars and merchandise weighing less than eight ounces. To be eligible for third-class rates the envelope or package may not be sealed.

THIRD-CLASS MAIL

Maximum 8 oz.

Advertising or other printed matter: 2¢ for first 2 oz. plus 1¢ for each additional oz.*

Books and catalogs of 24 pages or more: 2¢ for first 2 oz. plus 1½¢ for each additional 2 oz.*

PARCEL POST
(Fourth-Class Mail)

Any third-class matter weighing more than eight ounces, and not included in first- or second-class matter, is subject to parcel post (fourth-class) rates.

PARCEL POST

Rates vary with distance and weight. Check with post office.

CERTIFIED AND REGISTERED MAIL

Important documents such as contracts or other legal forms can be sent by Certified Mail. This service, which is available only on first-class matter, provides for a receipt to the sender and a record of delivery at the post office of the addressee.

Valuables, such as currency or jewelry, should be sent by registered mail. This service, which is available on first-, second-, and third-class mail, provides special safeguards to prevent loss.

CERTIFIED MAIL

20¢ **

REGISTERED MAIL

Value to $10 ....50¢ *
Value $10 to $100 ..75¢ *

For each additional $100 value, add 25¢.*

SPECIAL DELIVERY

To provide faster service and, within limitations, delivery by special messenger to the addressee, all classes of mail may be sent by special delivery.

SPECIAL DELIVERY

First class, air mail, or parcel post:

To 2 lbs. ....30¢ **
2 to 10 lbs. ....45¢ **
Over 10 lbs. ......60¢ **

Other classes:

To 2 lbs. ....45¢ **
2 to 10 lbs. ....55¢ **
Over 10 lbs. ......70¢ **

SPECIAL HANDLING

Parcel post packages can be sent by "special handling" and will be rushed to the Post Office of the addressee, but will not be delivered by special messenger.

SPECIAL HANDLING

To 2 lbs. ....25¢ **
2 to 10 lbs. ....35¢ **
Over 10 lbs. ......50¢ **

INSURED MAIL

Third- and fourth-class (parcel post) matter can be insured against loss up to a maximum of $200 per package. The insurance fee is based on the declared value of the package.

INSURED MAIL

Value to $10 ......10¢ **
Value $10 to $50 ..20¢ **
Value $50 to $100 .30¢ **
Value $100 to $200 .40¢**

RETURN RECEIPTS

If you wish to prove that an article was delivered, you can mark upon it "Return Receipt Requested." Any article sent by registered, certified, or insured mail can take advantage of this service.

RETURN RECEIPTS

Return receipt ....10¢ **

Return receipt showing address .....35¢ **

Return receipt on delivery restricted to one person ....50¢ **

COMMONLY MISSPELLED CITIES

Akron, Ohio
Annapolis, Maryland
Baton Rouge, Louisiana
Boise, Idaho
Chattanooga, Tennessee
Cheyenne, Wyoming
Cincinnati, Ohio
Des Moines, Iowa
Harrisburg, Pennsylvania
Houston, Texas

Indianapolis, Indiana
Juneau, Alaska
Milwaukee, Wisconsin
Montpelier, Vermont
Philadelphia, Pennsylvania
Phoenix, Arizona
Pierre, South Dakota
Pittsburgh, Pennsylvania
Tallahassee, Florida
Worcester, Massachusetts

STATE AND TERRITORY ABBREVIATIONS

Alabama	Ala.	Nebraska	Nebr.
Alaska, Territory of	Alaska	Nevada	Nev.
Arizona	Ariz.	New Hampshire	N. H.
Arkansas	Ark.	New Jersey	N. J.
California	Calif.	New Mexico	N. M.
Colorado	Colo.	New York	N. Y.
Connecticut	Conn.	North Carolina	N. C.
Delaware	Del.	North Dakota	N. D.
Florida	Fla.	Ohio	Ohio
Georgia	Ga.	Oklahoma	Okla.
Hawaii, Territory of	Hawaii	Oregon	Oreg.
Idaho	Idaho	Pennsylvania	Pa.
Illinois	Ill.	Puerto Rico, Territory of	P. R.
Indiana	Ind.	Rhode Island	R. I.
Iowa	Iowa	South Carolina	S. C.
Kansas	Kans.	South Dakota	S. D.
Kentucky	Ky.	Tennessee	Tenn.
Louisiana	La.	Texas	Tex.
Maine	Maine	Utah	Utah
Maryland	Md.	Vermont	Vt.
Massachusetts	Mass.	Virginia	Va.
Michigan	Mich.	Washington	Wash.
Minnesota	Minn.	West Virginia	W. Va.
Mississippi	Miss.	Wisconsin	Wis.
Missouri	Mo.	Wyoming	Wyo.
Montana	Mont.		

PROOFREADER'S MARKS

		EXAMPLE	
MARK	**MEANING**	**ERROR**	**CORRECTED**
[	Move to left.	[Dear Sir:	Dear Sir:
]	Move to right.	De]ar Sir:	Dear Sir:
‿	Close up.	ty‿ping	typing
∿ ⭜	Transpose.	in t⭜h⭜y ⭜.	in the
∧	Insert material.	refer∧ing	referring
ℓ	Take out; delete.	offerℓing	offering
#	Insert space.	you#may	you may
Cap or ≡	Change to a capital.	Cap dear ≡sir:	Dear Sir:
ℓ.c. or /	Change to a small letter.	My ℓ.c.Dear SIR:	My dear Sir:
stet	Let it stand.	We stet all hope	We all hope
¶	Paragraph.		

Before typing any rough drafts, always read ahead so that
you are prepared for any corrections.